G. McCann
Cambridge.

THE MOVIE MOGULS

THE MOVIE MOGULS

An Informal History of the Hollywood Tycoons

Philip French

Weidenfeld and Nicolson
5 Winsley Street London W1

To Kersti

SBN 297 76266 4

Printed in Great Britain by
Willmer Brothers Limited, Birkenhead

CONTENTS

ILLUSTRATIONS

AUTHOR'S PREFACE

This book was originally written at the suggestion of John Gross for the series he was editing called *Pageant of History*, where the film moguls would have rubbed shoulders (or nudged spines) – not altogether inappropriately – with other historical groups such as gladiators, highwaymen, gurkhas, assassins, gauchos, saints and the Bloomsbury set. Unfortunately, owing to a combination of my customary longwindedness and my poor arithmetic, the final manuscript proved roughly twice as long as that series could take and virtually irreducible. But the form of the book and my approach to the subject were dictated by the 'Pageant of History' idea. By this I mean three things.

First, this little monograph is neither a history of the American cinema nor a critical appraisal of its films: it concerns the men who superintended the fortunes of the eight major companies that rose to dominate the manufacture, distribution and exhibition of movies in America and a large part of the world. It is an account of their backgrounds, characters, tastes, business practices, attitudes and behaviour. And as I have dealt with them largely as a group, I have appended some biographical notes on the most important figures even though some of this material is to be found in the text. These notes, which I regard as an integral part of the book, can be read at any time after the first couple of chapters.

Secondly, *The Movie Moguls* is written not for cinema specialists but as a kind of social history for the general reader. (This isn't to say that I don't expect the former to find it of interest; in the course of preparing the book I learnt a great deal myself – among other things that one can put one's absolute trust in very few books on the cinema and must be wary of most reminiscences – and I'm constantly astonished by how little most serious moviegoers know of film history.) So I have included a brief overall history of the American cinema and the moguls' place in it. However, nowhere do I dwell much on statistics, the details of financial transactions and the complexities of corporate structures. To have done so would have taken up far more space than I had at my disposal, clogged up the narrative and demanded a firmer grasp upon business affairs than I possess.

Thirdly, such originality as this book might lay claim to resides in the way the material has been brought together: no similar study exists and there are at present available only two reliable biographies of movie moguls, one serious studio history, and no major history of Hollywood that covers the whole period from 1911 to the present day. I have conducted no original research, which is to say that the factual material contained here comes for the most part from the books listed at the back as well as from newspaper clippings and contemporary magazine articles. I am thus indebted, in greatly varying degree, to all the books mentioned, despite the rarity of specific citations in my text. I have never met in the flesh or been employed by any of the personalities discussed, though I have encountered over the years numerous artists who did know them and I have been influenced by what they told me of their Hollywood experiences. Los Angeles I have visited only twice and each time briefly. *The Movie Moguls* therefore makes no claims to being other than an outsider's view, though the view of an outsider who has been regularly exposed, along with most members of his generation the world over, to the moguls' products from a very early age.

Like anyone else in Britain writing on the cinema, I am grateful to the British Film Institute Library, without whose resources and ever-helpful staff this book could never have been written. I am also grateful to John Gross for encouraging me to complete a book that he suggested and that on several occasions I wished to abandon, and to my wife for abetting him in this pursuit and equally for her constant aid in helping to clarify my mind and prose.

I

UNSOLICITED TESTIMONIALS

His thoughts are seldom consecutive,
He just can write.
I know a movie executive
Who's twice as bright.
                    Lorenz Hart, *Pal Joey*

In the early 1930s there occurred within the space of a few months the deaths of Thomas Alva Edison, prolific inventor and movie pioneer, and his friend George Eastman, from whose Rochester, N.Y., laboratories came the first effective roll film. Both died rich in years and money, with a high place in the affections of their fellow countrymen. On the day of Edison's funeral millions of Americans, at the suggestion of President Hoover, briefly cut off their electricity as a final symbolic tribute to Edison's inventive genius.

Contemporaries, employees and so-called friends were less generous to the men who took the inventions of Edison and Eastman and developed them into one of the world's largest and most influential industries. After two thousand people had filled sound stages 12 and 14 (there is no 13) at Columbia studios to attend the gaudy 1958 funeral of Columbia's founder and president, Harry Cohn, the comedian Red Skelton remarked to a national television audience: 'Well, it only proves what they always say – give the public what they want to see, and they'll come out for it.' Of Louis B. Mayer, Samuel Goldwyn is reported to have said: 'The reason so many people showed up at his funeral was because they wanted to make sure he was dead.' The remark is probably apocryphal, for Mayer's funeral was poorly attended.

Of the typical movie tycoon, Ben Hecht (in his time the highest paid writer in Hollywood) wrote: 'He is usually a man who has no taste to be violated or distorted. He admires with his whole soul the drivel his underlings produce in his factory.' This view was shared by many who had never been near a film studio. When it was announced in 1930 that John Drinkwater was writing the official biography of film magnate Carl Laemmle, Sir Hugh Walpole wrote: 'I hope in changing from the Royal Navy of King Charles [Drinkwater's last book had been a life of Samuel Pepys] to the rich palaces of Hollywood, Mr Drinkwater will not lose his head', and he concluded his survey of forthcoming books by observing that 'of serious important biographies I see no sign'. On the same occasion E. V. Knox wrote a poem in *Punch* to the effect that he had never heard of Carl Laemmle.

In 1937 when Graham Greene attended a luncheon addressed by Louis B. Mayer to launch a series of M-G-M productions in Britain, he commented on the speaker's 'little level Jewish voice', and affected to hear a tribute to 'men like Eddy Sankatz' when Mayer had evidently referred to his two senior assistants Eddie Mannix and Sam Katz. Greene also mocked the presence on the top table of Sir Hugh Walpole who had lately returned from a lucrative expedition to Hollywood, the hospitality of whose rich palaces he had not spurned.

Contempt for these men comes easily, and the terms to describe them – mogul, cinemogul, tycoon, czar and the rest have a certain sneer about them, conjuring up as they do an unfavourable image of a cigar-chewing, language-fracturing, power-mad, philistine ignoramus. (By no accident these terms are also redolent of *Time* magazine which, being founded in 1923, grew up with Hollywood and coined 'cinemogul' – as well as 'cinemactor', 'cinemoppet', 'cinemaddict', etc. – and popularized the word 'tycoon'. Time Inc. itself is now a corporate cinemogul as the result of the organization's substantial holdings in Metro-Goldwyn-Mayer, a company that resulted from a complex merger that was being planned at the very moment the two recent Yale graduates, Henry Luce and Briton Hadden, were preparing to launch *Time the Weekly News-Magazine* from the same kind of humble Manhattan back-street premises out of which the movie business sprang a short while before.) This image unfortunately is not entirely without foundation in fact. Yet the easiness of this contempt is something to be guarded against, as Scott Fitzgerald recognized when he began to write *The Last Tycoon*. A dying man, a neglected artist, a Hollywood failure, Fitzgerald looked back to his first visit to California and the loathing he had for the movie industry, which he had partly worked out in his ambiguous story *Crazy Sunday*. And he wrote a working note for *The Last Tycoon*: 'Remember my summing up in *Crazy Sunday* – don't give the impression that these are bad people.' Then he went further with this comment by his narrator, the studio boss's daughter Cecilia, on the second page of the novel:

> You can take Hollywood for granted like I did, or you can dismiss it with the contempt we reserve for what we don't understand. It can be understood too, but only dimly and in flashes.

But old prejudices, especially those that contain an element of truth, die hard. Few people think as badly now of Hollywood films as contemporary critics did when they first appeared; the record is being revised as old films are constantly rediscovered and either elevated to classic status or at least seen as superior entertainments. Not that the reputations of the tycoons have benefited much from this process.[1] In many circles Hollywood still continues to be a blanket term for all that is most poisonous and debilitating, or at least dishonest and evasive, in mass culture. The criticism comes from left, right and centre. The classic case perhaps is that of T. S. Eliot's *The Cocktail Party* (1949), where Celia Coplestone goes out to far-off Kinganja as a missionary to keep her rendezvous with God by being crucified on an ant-hill while her boy-friend Peter Quilpe goes to work for the mogul Bela Szogody at Pan-Am-Eagle's Hollywood studio. 'I thought I had ideas to make a revolution/ In the cinema that

---

[1] A rare exception is to be found in Gore Vidal's scintillating novel *Myra Breckinridge*, the greatest testimonial to Hollywood ever made by a member of what the *New Yorker* writer Roger Angell dubbed 'the movie generation'. Believing that 'between 1935 and 1945, no irrelevant film was made in the United States', Myra is a passionate devotee of the mythic qualities of American stars and movies. To Myra, Metro-Goldwyn-Mayer's Culver City is 'the Studio of Studios, the sublime motor of this century's myths', and she throws special bouquets to her favourite M-G-M producers, Sam Zimbalist and Pandro S. Berman.

3

no one could ignore – / And here I am, making a second-rate film!', the poor fellow cries. A more extreme instance is to be found from the left: on his return a couple of years ago to the Soviet Union after three years in America, Albertas Laurinchukas, correspondent of *Selskaya Zhrn,* reported:

All the propaganda of the capitalist world is saturated with a scandalous and piquant, mysterious and glittering, enticing and murderous elixir called Hollywood ... Hollywood is the world's largest factory of filth, where there is no room for dreams. People there smile only when the camera lights are turned on.

Rail as he will, Laurinchukas would have to admit, as would more temperate critics, that when given the opportunity the mass audiences of the world generally voted with their feet at the box office in favour of the products of the Hollywood dream factory rather than for their native offerings.

The only reference to Hollywood I have found in the whole twenty years of F. R. Leavis's *Scrutiny* is altogether more reasonable than Laurinchukas's outburst and a good deal less patronising than *Scrutiny*'s one-time hero, T. S. Eliot. It occurs in a 1939 review by W. H. Mellers of *The Fifth Column* where Hollywood is used as a rod to chastise Ernest Hemingway, who oddly enough was among the few American writers who resolutely refused to have anything to do with the commercial cinema (and in this respect at least stands in marked contrast to Henry James, whose attempts to succeed in the West End theatre of his time make a pathetic story). In his *Scrutiny* essay entitled *Hollywood-Hero,* Mellers writes:

In saying that [*A Farewell to Arms*] is accomplished I mean that it is competent with the slickness of the tougher type of Hollywood film. It is often said that Hollywood emotion is essentially synthetic but this, though true, is not the whole truth. It is wrong to assume that glycerine tears, because they are often inadequately motivated and always unsubtle, because they lack sensibility and hence any of the real passion that cannot exist apart from sensibility, have therefore no motivation at all; it is wrong to put all the blame on Hollywood for tapping the glycerine vats in people's hearts and none on people for possessing those vats waiting to be tapped at; and we must

4

remember, too, that though there is much that is deliberately vicious in glycerine tears, yet a form of art or entertainment so popular and universal cannot exist without incarnating, even if fortuitously, some of the values which the people who patronise it honestly live by.[2]

This judgment is far from being unjust, especially considering that the source of these remarks was never celebrated for its fairness.

[2]*Scrutiny*, Vol. VIII, 1939. Reprinted in *A Selection from Scrutiny*, Vol. II, edited by F. R. Leavis, Cambridge University Press, 1968, p. 90.

2

THE BACKGROUND

What is the future of the kinetograph?
Ask rather, from what conceivable phase
of the future can it be debarred.
           W. K. L. Dickson, 1896

No person can truly be said to have invented the motion picture, though for many years the credit, in America at least, was given to Thomas Edison who had after all invented nearly everything else, from the phonograph to the electric light. It was the outcome of years of speculation, investigation and tinkering; in the second half of the nineteenth century people throughout the world were working towards the same end, and Europe is rich in plaques commemorating the birthplaces of various competing 'fathers of cinematography'. But the best known of the early devices was Edison's kinetoscope which enabled short reels of film to be viewed through a peep-hole and proved an exciting novelty in the amusement arcades of the early 1890s. This by-product of the phonograph struck Edison at the time as being among the least of his achievements. The real breakthrough came in 1895 with the discovery of a means of projecting the film onto a screen, thus making possible the gathering of an audience, the economic basis of an industry. It also made extended viewing feasible, though considerable improvements in the quality of projection and film stock were needed before feature-length films could be produced: this equally required an imaginative leap by movie-makers and the acceptance by producers that audiences would – and physically could – regularly endure a single picture that lasted an hour or more.

A patent in a version of this particular innovation was acquired by the Edison company mainly through the enthusiasm of the great man's associates. The most notable of them, an Englishman,

1 Douglas Fairbanks, Mary Pickford, Charlie Chaplin and D. W. Griffith who after World War I formed United Artists to make and distribute their own movies. They evoked from Richard Rowland, head of production at Metro Pictures, the famous remark: 'The lunatics have taken charge of the asylum'.

2 Fred Niblo, director of the silent *Ben Hur*, with his employer, Louis B. Mayer (right), and (centre) Mayer's future boss, Marcus Loew, creator of Loew's Inc. and Metro-Goldwyn-Mayer. A picture taken in 1923 on the set of *The Famous Mrs Fair*, a Mayer film released by Loew's Metro company before the 1924 M-G-M merger.

3 The dapper William Fox, the former 'pants presser' who successfully defied the Motion Picture Trust and set up the Fox Film Corporation He was ousted from this and spent the last twenty years of his life in the wilderness.

4 Impresario Jesse L. Lasky, actor-director Cecil B. DeMille and one-time glove salesman Samuel Goldfish (later Goldwyn) in 1916 at the time of the merger of their Lasky Feature Plays company with Adolph Zukor's Famous Players.

5 The Brothers Warner in their less affluent days, before talking pictures brought them prosperity as well as illuminated addresses and signed photographs to cover the walls. Left to right: Producer Harry Rapf, Sam, Harry, Jack and Albert Warner. In the early twenties Rapf was lured away by Louis Mayer and remained with M-G-M until his death in 1949.

6 Thomas Alva Edison, inventor and national hero, poses with Adolph Zukor on the latter's night of triumph – the official opening of the palatial Paramount Theatre in Times Square, New York, 19 November 1926.

7 The diminutive 'Uncle Carl' Laemmle, the former Oshkosh, Wisconsin, store-keeper and founder of Universal Pictures, partnered not by one of his window dummies but by Priscilla Dean, star of numerous Universal movies of the immediate post World War I years.

8 William Fox, with the inevitable cigar and air of concentration, conducting his world-wide business from his own back-yard.

9 The 23-year-old furrier and prospective film magnate Adolph Zukor in 1896, accompanied by one of his pelts. It was his adroitness in tailoring and marketing furs that had led to the accumulation of a modest fortune since his arrival in America seven years before.

The Background

William Kennedy Laurie Dickson, wrote in his pamphlet, *History of the Photographic and Scientific Experiments and Developments Leading up to the Perfection of the Vitascope* (1896):

It is the crown and flower of nineteenth century magic, the crystallisation of Eons of groping enchantments. In its wholesome, sunny and accessible laws are possibilities undreamt of by the occult lore of the East: the conservative wisdom of Egypt, the jealous erudition of Babylon, the guarded mysteries of Delphic and Eleusinian shrines. It is the earnest of the coming age, when the great potentialities of life shall no longer be in the keeping of cloister and college or money bag, but shall overflow to the nethermost portions of the earth at the command of the humblest heir of the divine intelligence.

In this strange mixture of accurate and erroneous prophecy, Dickson anticipated more the tone of movie advertising than subsequent industrial history. (But we must not forget that this book is concerned only with the world of the entertainment film and not the scientific, educational and other aspects of the cinema which are quite as, if not more, important.) Yet those who saw the moving picture as merely a novelty for the burgeoning, illiterate immigrant masses, a fad that would soon pass, were also mistaken. After the turn of the century the fad remained, despite periods of recession. Little store-front cinemas opened all over America; films were shown between vaudeville acts and as 'chasers' to get people out of the theatre; and mobile booths travelled with fairs. 'Exchanges' grew up at major regional centres: at first to swop films informally, then, as distribution agencies, to hire them out. A major contributory factor to this growth was the sudden appearance on the market of cheap second-hand projectors that had been bought by vaudeville houses to fill in during an actors' strike and dispensed with when the live performers went back to work. The films shown were brief and crude, but ever improving, particularly the French imports; programmes changed daily; admission was cheap – usually five cents. The term 'nickelodeon' caught on from the first cinema given this name in Pennsylvania in 1905. Dozens of firms, mostly of a fly-by-night character, sprang up to satisfy the voracious demand, and business practices were sharp. Films were copied and pirated, false returns made to distributors ('bicycling' was the name given to the illicit system of speeding a print from the cinema that had hired it to other cinemas that had not); crude makeshift machines were constructed from the Edison and foreign models. Civic bodies became disturbed both by the insanitary conditions of picture houses and by what might be going on there in the dark. Lawyers took to blaming the movies for the depredations of their juvenile clients. Accidents were frequent – from overcrowding and from fires due to unsafe machines and inflammable celluloid.

As fortunes large and small were being made, disputes arose between the holders of patents to various aspects of film-making equipment and projecting machines. While these were contested in the courts and the confused history of invention was argued at great legal expense, the more established companies decided to quit the courts and consolidate in one overall combination to monopolize the business. As this monopoly would be based on patents their organization would, they thought, avoid the Sherman Anti-Trust Act. So in 1908 the Edison, Biograph, Vitagraph, Lubin, Selig, Essanay, and Kalem companies came together with the French firms Pathé and Méliès to form the Motion Pictures Patent Company. The aim was to control across America and throughout Europe the production, distribution and exhibition of all films. The Company had an exclusive contract for raw stock with Eastman Kodak, granted licences to exhibitors at two dollars a week for each projector, and sold films, irrespective of quality, at ten cents a foot through licensed film exchanges. Initially the Patent Company was a success under the leadership of a tough Irish ex-construction boss, Jeremiah J. Kennedy; exhibitors signed up or got out of business. But opposition soon made itself felt, and as it grew the Patent Company backed up its battery of lawyers, who were fighting the outlaw companies in the courts, with less orthodox methods. Goon squads, every bit as vicious as the professional strike-breakers then being hired by American industrialists, were dispatched to smash illegal equipment, intimidate unlicensed film-makers and disrupt their activities.

But Kennedy underrated his opposition as much as the Patent Company overrated the validity of its patents and its immunity from the Anti-Trust Laws. The Sherman Act of 1890 was designed to support the small entrepreneur against the giant monopolies, and when Woodrow Wilson was elected president in 1912 the Patent Company looked, and was, the sort of relatively small organization that might be proceeded against to compensate for the government's continuing failure to hit the really big trusts. The battle however was lost before the matter had dragged its way through the courts – and it was lost because of the multiplicity of the opposition, the ingenuity and resilience of its leaders, and because the Patent Company stood in the way of inevitable progress. The principal heroes of the 'Independents', as the outlaws called themselves, were the exchange owners and exhibitors Carl Laemmle and William Fox. In Chicago Laemmle stood firm in the face of a dozen threats and a hundred writs and rallied his supporters with a brilliant campaign of ridicule in the press, masterminded by his publicity adviser Robert H. Cochrane; in New York, William Fox hung on to his film exchange and got himself some good lawyers and influential political connections. Both started making their own pictures when supplies were cut off, and they and others raided the licensed production companies to acquire established talent whom they rewarded with money and the innovation of screen credits, a practice the Patent Company had frowned on. Then Adolph Zukor, a licensed exhibitor, persuaded the Patent Company to let him import a European feature film, *Queen Elizabeth,* which proved a success when shown under circumstances more like the legitimate theatre to attract the carriage trade. But when he sought Patent Company support in making such lengthy pictures locally they refused to co-operate. Zukor was thus driven into the ranks of the Independents.

By 1912 'The Trust' (as the Independents had dubbed the Patent Company) had its back to the wall, by 1913 it was on its last legs, and by the time it was officially declared a Trust four years later all that remained was to prepare its business arm and principal distributing agency, the General Film Company, for the official receiver.

While this struggle ensued film-makers had begun to move away from New York, trying Cuba, Florida, Chicago, St Louis and southern California. And increasingly the activities of both outlaws and licensed companies focused on Los Angeles and environs, which offered many attractions: cheap real estate, a co-operative chamber of commerce, the sun (an essential technical requirement at the time), diversity of landscape, and, for the 'Independents', the remoteness from the Patent Company's New York headquarters and the proximity of the Mexican border should the Trust's long arm stretch out to them. By 1920 the west coast was the pre-eminent production centre and has remained, despite occasional competition from elsewhere, the world's largest congregation of film-making talent if not always the most prolific producer of films. The generic term for this production centre became Hollywood, though only two important companies now have their actual studios in this north-western suburb of Los Angeles. Hollywood was named in the 1880s by one of its first settlers, a Mrs Horace H. Wilcox from Kansas (the family's own name lives on in Wilcox Boulevard), who took the name from a Chicago friend's summer residence. It was incorporated as a city in 1903, but in 1910, with a population of 4,000, the inadequacy of local water supplies compelled the residents to forsake their city status and become a district of Los Angeles. (The population of Hollywood itself is now around 200,000.) Even before that time some film-making had been done in the area, and in 1911 the short-lived Nestor Company built the first Hollywood studio. The accidental choice by Cecil B. De-Mille of a barn at what is now a block from Hollywood Boulevard and Vine Street to make *The Squaw Man* in 1913 means that of the major studios Paramount first put down its roots in Hollywood's arid soil. That barn became an official State historical monument and has a revered place on the Paramount lot. As this book is not exactly filled with accounts of kind acts or disinterested generosity, it might be worth mentioning here the extraordinary action of the self-made Polish immigrant Sigmund 'Pop' Lubin, a leading Philadelphia exhibitor and one of the Patent Company's founders. Due to his almost total ignorance of movie-making, DeMille returned to the East with an unshowable version of *The Squaw Man*. Faced with the possibility that their investment had gone down the drain and that they would have to repay advances made on the film, DeMille and his partners (Jesse Lasky and Samuel Goldwyn) threw themselves on the mercy of Lubin. With apparently little to gain from assisting these tyros, Lubin put his assistants to work on the picture and they soon discovered a minor error (the sprocket holes in the film had been incorrectly punched) that they were able to correct, although it could easily have been represented to the producers as beyond redemption, and might have been so by anyone else. Lubin's personal empire began to crumble shortly afterwards and he died in 1923 a relatively poor man; this astonishingly benevolent gesture should ensure that he is not forgotten.

As a consequence of its becoming the centre of movie activity, Hollywood also became, and remained, the principal focus of the West Coast radio and television industry. But the word Hollywood, as well as meaning the film industry in California, also became a general term, as I have already indicated, for the commercial American-dominated cinema everywhere, and the state of mind and nexus of attitudes that it supposedly induces.

With the coming of the first world war the European cinema went into a steep decline: America was thus able not only to draw abreast but to take a decisive lead. The emphasis was still on one- and two-reelers lasting up to twenty minutes, the great decade of the Keystone comedies and of Charlie Chaplin. However, the activities of Cecil B. DeMille and Adolph Zukor and above all the fantastic commercial success of D. W. Griffith's *Birth of a Nation* in 1915 proved that the industrial future of the cinema lay in the European-pioneered full-length feature film. While it was still possible technically for movies to be made for extremely small sums, the cost of production rose astronomically over a period of five years, due partly to public demand for higher quality staging and a move towards grandiose projects on a Griffithian scale, but mainly to the vast salaries, up to a million dollars a year, being demanded and obtained by newly-created stars such as Mary Pickford and Charlie Chaplin.

The 1920s was a period of consolidation, with the linking of manufacture, distribution and exhibition into larger units. Moving from opposite ends of the business, producers continued to buy up film exchanges and cinemas to ensure an outlet for their products and theatre owners acquired production companies to guarantee a regular supply of films at reasonable rentals. In the early 1920s the cinema again became the focus of attacks by puritanical groups alarmed by the allegedly immoral content of pictures and the dubious conduct of the now widely publicized people who made them. As the threat of censorship loomed and foreign countries began erecting barriers against American films, the leaders of the industry formed the Motion Picture Producers and Distributors Association of America to present a unified face to the public, and to impose some order upon the general muddle that had resulted from such swift growth. With Will H. Hays as its first president, the MPPDA proved extremely effective. A minor panic occasioned by the advent of radio was followed by the industry's second principal crisis of the 'twenties: the conversion to sound. The tycoons had already gone cap in hand to the bankers during the period of post-war expansion to meet increasing production costs and to finance their chains of super cinemas. Now fresh capital was needed to re-equip the studios and movie palaces for sound. The expensive transition to talking films was under way when the Wall Street crash occurred, an event whose impact was initially delayed but which eventually rocked the rickety empires, affecting box-office takings, shaking industrial morale and weakening even further the tycoons' grasp on their own business. By 1935 the industry was dominated by eight giant corporations, their administrative headquarters in New York, their film-making activities in Hollywood, and their ultimate fate in the hands of outside financiers. There were still many small companies, but these were known collectively as 'Poverty

Row', the name used thirty years before to describe the whole chaotic appearance of the Hollywood movie-making area.

By the late 'thirties it was clear that the industry was beginning to break down – or more accurately that it could not totter precariously on in the same confused way for much longer. Independent production, deliberately stifled ten years before, and not the studio factory was to be the pattern of the future. The second world war postponed the day of reckoning and ushered in the big studios' period of greatest prosperity. The war put off the imminent threat of television and provided domestic and foreign audiences (large enough to more than compensate for the loss of the continental European market) so hungry for diversion that it was difficult to make a film that did not show a handsome profit. The result was that when the war ended several blows struck a complacent industry geared to over-production. The biggest blow was television, which steadily eroded the regular undiscriminating weekly audience – as Sam Goldwyn said: 'Who wants to go out and see a bad movie when they can stay at home and see a bad one free on television?' The process began a couple of years after the war in the big cities, rapidly accelerating during the early 'fifties until by the late 'fifties a virtual saturation point in coverage and possession of sets had been reached. Apart from television there was competition for the public's time from the dozens of other leisure activities that had sprung up in an increasingly affluent society, not to mention the ex-urban drift that has been a major feature of post-war American life (even if this development has been partially met by the drive-in cinema[1]). Moreover studio overheads were too high and production costs had soared. Nevertheless, individual movies continued to make more money than ever. Then came the culmination of the Depart-

[1]The economic influence of the drive-in is not easy to calculate but in the first ten post-war years when a third of America's twenty thousand odd cinemas closed, over five thousand drive-ins opened. Certainly several Hollywood directors have told me that technical standards in some studio laboratories have taken drive-in exhibition into account, just as more recently the standard of colour films has been affected by colour television. At drive-ins, even more than normal cinemas, a high proportion of the total profits, something probably in excess of forty per cent, comes from the sale of confectionery, ice-cream, hot-dogs, soft drinks and so on.

ment of Justice's anti-trust investigation that had been hanging over the industry since the early 'twenties. Initiated in a serious way in 1938 and vigorously pursued from 1945 after a wartime moratorium, the action was directed against restrictive trade practices such as block booking, admission price fixing, theatre pooling agreements and other coercive or apparently conspiratorial activities, and against the allegedly monopolistic situation of a single company manufacturing and distributing movies *and* owning cinemas. In 1948, all the companies agreed to abandon the restrictive practices, which let the 'little Three' – Universal, Columbia and United Artists – out of the case as they owned few movie houses; and by 1952 Loew's, the last of the so-called 'Big Five' cinema-owning producer-distributors, entered into a consent decree, as RKO, Paramount, Warner Brothers and Twentieth Century-Fox had done before them, by which the company agreed to divorce the manufacture and distribution of movies from their exhibition. Complicated schemes of divestiture were arranged, with the whole operation to be completed by the mid-fifties. So the giants were cloven in twain, the studios and their distribution outfits going off in one direction and the theatre chains in another, as separate companies. The day of the big organizations was not over, but they were never to function in the same way again.

Over the years the names of these companies have become famous all round the globe, their trademarks stamping themselves on the international consciousness as week after week they have appeared on the screens of the world heralding the company's latest offerings – or increasingly in the last fifteen years on the small screen. Everyone recognizes these signs though what lies behind them is as little known as the functions performed by those named in the lengthy list of credits which they precede: the Metro-Goldwyn-Mayer lion beneath the ironic motto *Ars Gratia Artis*; the searchlights raking the constructivist-expressionist townscape made up of the title Twentieth Century-Fox; the radio-mast atop the world signalling the arrival of a picture from RKO Radio (later reduced to a formal inverted-triangle device shot through with a streak of lightning); the sedately draped Statue of Liberty figure holding aloft her torch for Columbia; the turning sphere with a ring of Saturn spelling out 'Universal' (subsequently a more orthodox moving globe with the title 'Universal-International' imposed); the shield containing the letters WB suggesting the Warner Brothers flashing their official badge of 'good films and good citizenship'; the cool, anonymous lozenge enclosing the words 'United Artists'; the fuzzy, star-spangled, snow-capped mountain of Paramount.

The origins of these companies are immensely complicated, the results of numerous mergers, and each contains, or contained, many subsidiaries. Moreover top executives shifted from one corporation to another with great frequency, and several played a part in the founding of more than one studio.

Universal, the oldest, was formed when several independent companies opposing the Trust came together in 1912 under the leadership of Carl Laemmle, who remained its nominal head until he was pushed out by banking interests three years before his death in 1939. In the 'forties the company merged with, or rather took over, International Pictures, a small company run by William Goetz, to become Universal-International. The title Universal was inspired by a van labelled Universal Pipe Fittings that Laemmle spotted from a window during a crucial board meeting. In 1951 Decca Records acquired a substantial interest in the company which became a controlling one when they purchased the stock that the British J. Arthur Rank Organization had held since 1946. Ten years later the Music Corporation of America Inc., the vast artists' agency and television film production company, consolidated with Decca to make Universal the theatrical film producing side of its operation. Later MCA was forced to abandon its agency work to concentrate on film production for cinemas and television.

The Fox company dates from around the same time and took the name of its founder William Fox when his enterprises were consolidated in 1915. Fox was driven out of the company in 1931, and in 1935, still in a bad way, its extensive chains of cinemas and Hollywood production lot were merged with Twentieth Century Pictures, a bustling new studio started in 1933 by Darryl F. Zanuck and Joseph Schenck.

Paramount takes its name from a distribution company started in 1915 by an ex-Patent Company exchange operator, W. W. Hodkinson, who borrowed the title from an apartment house and himself sketched the trademark on a paper napkin. It specialized in distributing the pictures of two companies formed in 1913: Adolph Zukor's Famous Players and Lasky Feature Plays (organized by Samuel Goldwyn, Jesse L. Lasky and Cecil B. DeMille). These two united as Famous Players-Lasky in 1916 and shortly afterwards took over their distributor and absorbed some dozen smaller production companies. From 1919 onwards Zukor conducted a vigorous programme of theatre acquisition and building until by the late 'twenties the company had control of, or a major interest in, over six hundred movie houses, including the Chicago-based chain of the Balaban family and Sam Katz, who came into the company on the exhibition side. (Paramount thus went ahead of, and was rivalled only by, the cinema holdings of Fox and Loew's Inc. and later Warners.) The names Paramount, for the distribution of films, Famous Players-Lasky for the production of pictures in Hollywood and at the firm's Long Island studio (the latter was closed down in the 'thirties), and Publix for the exhibition, were kept separate for a while. The company subsequently changed its name to Paramount-Famous-Lasky (1927), next to Paramount-Publix (1930), and then from the 1930s went through several variations on Paramount (e.g. Paramount Productions Inc., Paramount Pictures Inc.) before becoming in 1951 two separate companies – Paramount Pictures Corporation for production and distribution, the United Paramount Theatres Inc. (with control over 867 cinemas) for exhibition. The alteration to Paramount Pictures Inc. in 1935 came when the company was reorganized after two years of bankruptcy, with Barney Balaban becoming president, another former exhibitor, Y. Frank Freeman (a native of Georgia who like Balaban had brought his Southern circuit into the Paramount orbit in the 'twenties), appointed vice-president in charge of production, and Adolph Zukor retained as chairman of the board. In 1966, Paramount merged with, and thus became a subsidiary of, the giant Gulf and Western Industries.

United Artists was formed in 1919 by Charles Chaplin, Mary Pickford, Douglas Fairbanks and D. W. Griffith. The suggestion that they form a company to exploit their own talent (which few studios could afford anyway) was made to them by Oscar Price when they were together on a bond-selling tour during the first world war. Price was publicity assistant to William Gibbs McAdoo Secretary of the Treasury in his father-in-law Woodrow Wilson's cabinet, and later one of California's senators. Price became the company's first president, but left soon afterwards along with McAdoo who had become associated with the company after the initial meeting to found it had been held at his home. He was followed by the former head of Paramount, Hiram Abrams, and Joseph Schenck. In the mid-twenties Adolph Zukor is said to have made overtures to the company, and at one point a projected merger with M-G-M was prevented by Chaplin's refusal to agree to the move. Another former Paramount executive, the Hungarian-born one-time movie-house usher Al Lichtman, succeeded Schenck; he left in 1935 to join M-G-M (the Metro part of which had grown out of his failed Alco Company) and finished up as vice-president of Loew's Inc. On his retirement from Loew's in 1949, the ubiquitous Lichtman at the age of sixty-one joined Twentieth Century-Fox as distribution manager. For a couple of years after Lichtman's departure, United Artists was run jointly by the Californian banker A. H. Giannini and George Schaefer (one-time secretary to Lewis Selznick and later president of RKO). Throughout the 'thirties, Samuel Goldwyn was a United Artists stockholder, as was for a while the Hungarian-born British producer-director Alexander Korda. The company was not in fact a studio but an organization that existed to hire studios (though most of the more prominent people connected with it had their own) and to distribute the work of independent producers who made insufficient films to warrant their own national or world-wide sales operation. The company owned few cinemas, never fulfilling its original intention of operating a major chain. Moreover Griffith left early on and

Chaplin, switching to full-length feature films in the early 'twenties, made a mere seven pictures for United Artists' release in thirty years. In 1950, Mary Pickford and Charles Chaplin sold all but a handful of their shares to a short-lived syndicate that gave way to another more enduring one run by the New York lawyers Arthur B. Krim and Robert Benjamin (both of whom had been partners of Louis Nizer, a major legal adviser to the industry and America's greatest trial lawyer), and Max Youngstein, a former vice-president of Paramount. Together they brought United Artists out of the doldrums. The company is now part of the vast TransAmerica Corporation.

The firm of Warner Brothers dates from the early 'twenties, its founders Harry, Albert, Sam and Jack Warner having begun their careers as exhibitors and distributors early in the century. They took over two ailing corporations that had been major forces in the industry when the Warners were operating on the fringe – Vitagraph, one of the Patent Company members, which was absorbed in 1924, and the once powerful First National in 1929. The First National Exhibitors Circuit had been formed in 1917 when a group of prosperous cinema-owners moved into production, and the Warner Brothers were able to acquire this once powerful outfit and its numerous cinemas as a result of their success with sound movies. Two years ago the independent company Seven Arts took over Warners, and now the company is called 'Warner-7 Arts' with a W-7 colophon after the style of, though aesthetically far less satisfying than, the original design.

Metro-Goldwyn-Mayer was a triple merger engineered in 1924 by Marcus Loew to serve as the production arm of Loew's Inc. of New York, an extensive chain of cinemas and vaudeville houses. Loew had established his own company initially as a vaudeville circuit before the first world war in association with Adolph Zukor, and the brothers Joseph and Nicholas Schenck. He had acquired the troubled Metro company in 1920 to ensure a supply of films for his own cinemas. The Goldwyn company had been formed in 1916 by the Selwyn Brothers and Sam Goldwyn. (Goldwyn had quit Famous Players-Lasky shortly after its formation and was, despite his financial holding, no longer active in the Goldwyn company at the time of the merger.) The Mayer studio had been set up in Los Angeles in 1919 by Louis B. Mayer, a former New England exhibitor. M-G-M remained the production unit of the parent company Loew's Inc. until the 1950s. Mayer was in charge of production up to 1951, and Nicholas Schenck became president of Loew's on the death of Marcus Loew in 1927.

Columbia was also formed in 1924, but took some time to drag its way from Poverty Row to major status. It was the creation of Joe Brandt and the brothers Jack and Harry Cohn, all three former employees of Carl Laemmle, and grew from their earlier CBC Company which had specialized in making and distributing low budget films. Harry Cohn was head of production and (from 1932) also president until his death in 1958.

RKO Radio Pictures has perhaps the most complicated history of all, involving dozens of mergers dating back to before the first world war. In the form in which the organization became prominent, RKO was the creation of the Boston banker Joseph Kennedy. He brought together his own Film Booking Office of America first with the Keith, Albee and Orpheum theatre circuits and then with the Radio Corporation of America which was attracted into films with the coming of sound. The studio underwent several changes of ownership in the 'thirties (for a period it was part of the Rockefeller empire), and like both Paramount and Fox was for a time in the hands of trustees. After the second world war it was acquired by Howard Hughes who retained control for nearly ten years until 1957 when he sold off its back list of movies to television and the studio itself to the Desilu television company.

Of the numerous other concerns the only company to approach the eight 'majors' (the 'Big Five' and the 'Little Three' as they were before the Justice Department evened things out) was Republic Pictures, the creation of Herbert Yates (1880-1966), a former tobacco salesman who came into movies through backing independent film production before the first world war and running processing laboratories. Republic was formed by a merger of four independent companies in the early 'thirties and operated from Mack Sennett's former studio. The company specialized in B-feature Westerns (particularly the singing variety), thrillers and serials until the late 'forties and early 'fifties when it entered major features production. Somehow Republic never quite made the grade. However large the budget, the results always looked like inflated B-movies, though it achieved some renown by backing and distributing some films of John Ford's Argosy Pictures, most notably the 1952 Academy Award winner *The Quiet Man*. And occasionally the studio came up with a bizarre sport like Nicholas Ray's celebrated *Johnny Guitar* (1954). More than anything else Republic is remembered for the frequent starring vehicles provided for the Czech skating star Vera Hubra Ralston (runner-up to Sonja Henie in the 1936 Olympics) whose sole quality off the ice was a sense of chilly detachment. After declaring their unwavering devotion to her, many a Republic hero went off to face Indian arrows or Axis artillery, and invariably with a desperation born of disbelief. Miss Ralston happened to be the wife of President Herbert Yates (and forty years his junior), a source of much amusement to the Hollywood community and some consternation to Republic stockholders, as her movies almost consistently showed indifferent returns at the box-office. As Miss Ralston lacked the *brio* of Marion Davies and her husband could hardly lay claim to the charisma of William Randolph Hearst, their professional association must remain a rather pathetic, if touching, footnote to the present story. Anyway, in 1957 Republic abandoned the production and distribution of movies for the cinema and its studio switched to the manufacture of television films.

3

CHANCE AND CHUTZPAH

Those of us who became film producers hailed
from all sorts of occupations – furriers, magicians,
butchers, boilermakers – and for this reason
highbrows have often poked fun at us. Yet one
thing is certain – every man who succeeded was a
born showman. And once he was in the show business
he was never happy out of it.

Adolph Zukor

The founders of the American film industry were mainly immigrants or the sons of immigrants who arrived in America from
central and eastern Europe during the mass immigration of the
late nineteenth century. Carl Laemmle, Samuel Goldwyn and
Adolph Zukor arrived alone as teenagers; William Fox and
Louis B. Mayer passed through New York's Castle Garden immigration station as small children; Harry Warner was born in
Poland, while his three younger brothers were born in different
North American towns as their father travelled as a pedlar.

Not all of them were immigrants and not all of them were
Jews. There were Irish-Americans like Eddie Mannix, Mayer's
right hand man at M-G-M, and Winfield Sheehan, who joined
William Fox from the New York police department and rose to
be vice-president. The Skouras brothers were Greek peasants
who started out as waiters in St Louis hotels and finished up as
millionaire theatre-owners. Sidney Kent, the Nebraskan railroad worker who preceded Spyros Skouras as Fox president, the
Utah correspondence-school salesman W. W. Hodkinson, who
named Paramount, and a few others were native Americans of
British descent. But the majority were of orthodox Jewish parentage – of the eight major companies six can be said to be substantially or entirely of Jewish foundation and Jews played an important role at most stages in the development of the other two,
RKO and United Artists. Zukor's mother was a Hungarian
rabbi's daughter and his brother became a distinguished rabbi in

Germany; Louis B. Mayer's father was a Hebraic scholar, and so on. There are few instances of movie tycoons adhering to the orthodox faith, but none utterly repudiated it.

They came to America in search of opportunity: to escape the grinding poverty their families had endured for generations, to flee the oppressive life of the ghetto and the Jewish pale. 'I arrived from Hungary an orphan boy of sixteen with a few dollars sewn inside my vest,' wrote Zukor in 1953, at the age of eighty. 'I was thrilled to breathe the fresh strong air of freedom and America has been good to me.' America was no doubt preferable to Hungary, yet 1889 was perhaps not the best year to arrive. The frontier had closed, the country was on the verge of a serious recession, unemployment was widespread, and the White Anglo-Saxon Protestant establishment was beginning to be afflicted with a strong attack of xenophobia. Earlier in the century when the total Jewish community – mainly of German origin – numbered some one hundred and fifty thousand, anti-semitism scarcely existed; Jews were readily accepted in the best society, admitted to exclusive clubs, and assimilated into communities without needing to forsake their religious and dietary practices. With the mass immigration from eastern Europe the situation suddenly changed. The 'poor huddled masses yearning to breathe free', so amply welcomed by the verses of the Jewish poet Emma Lazarus on the Statue of Liberty (Miss Lazarus incidentally was the first Jew Ralph Waldo Emerson had ever met), found themselves huddled into ghettoes only too reminiscent of the ones they had left, subjected to exclusion and insult, denied the promise of the land of opportunity; or at least forced to fight for their share of that promise. There was nothing gentlemanly or clandestine about many manifestations of this anti-semitism. Before the first world war George S. Kauffman, soon to become Broadway's blue-chip playwright and a successful screenwriter, was fired from a Washington newspaper when its proprietor, the egregious Frank Munsey, spotted him sitting there: 'Who hired that Jew?' shouted Munsey. The great Henry Ford himself was a prominent publisher of anti-semitic literature and was largely responsible for initiating the American vogue of that infamous forgery 'The Protocols of the Elders of Zion'. Admittedly Ford in his old age became a good friend of Louis B. Mayer, and anti-semitism over the years took on a less virulent cast without ever completely disappearing. The Warner brothers, for instance, were denied membership of the Los Angeles country club across the road from their studio and were forced to contact their employees there by telephone. Their Jewishness made the tycoons the target for rabble-rousers and racists, and gave them a permanent sense of insecurity. It also contributed towards their enormous drive to succeed, to drag themselves out of the ghetto.

'I determined then and there that I would get out of my environment. It became my one motivating force,' said Sam Katz, the son of a poor immigrant Russian barber in Chicago. And for Katz, growing up after the turn of the century, the cinema already existed; at thirteen he was playing the piano in one of Carl Laemmle's nickelodeons, and was soon operating his own chain of cinemas. He also worked his way through Northwestern University and thus belonged to a very small handful of movie executives born in the nineteenth century who received a college education. Most of these were lawyers, such as J. Robert Rubin, a well-established New York attorney who joined M-G-M after serving as legal adviser to both Loew and Mayer, and Saul Rogers, the subtle mind who helped Fox in his battle against the Trust. The others lacked not merely a university degree; they had almost no education at all. After a few years of primary schooling they were forced out into full-time employment to help support their large and impoverished families. Laemmle, Fox and and the Warner brothers all came from families of twelve children, and an unsuccessful father appears to have been almost a necessary condition for a successful movie magnate.

Before he left school to join his father in the garment industry, William Fox had been selling stove-blacking door-to-door, hiring umbrellas to theatre patrons, and organizing fellow urchins to peddle cough lozenges, an activity that brought him into the courts. Marcus Loew had been selling newspapers at the age of six and left school at nine to work in various East Side sweatshops. Of the early group, the only ones to continue their education as teenagers were the immigrants like Zukor and Goldwyn who attended night-school to learn English; for this reason the Rockefeller Foundation could scarcely have chosen a more sympathetic sociologist than Leo Rosten, the creator of the immigrant night-school hero Hyman Kaplan, to head its three-year investigation of Hollywood that resulted in the publication of *Hollywood: The Movie Colony, the Moviemakers*.

They all passed from job to job, usually in some field connected with sales, and had a good share of failure and frustration. The furrier Marcus Loew had twice gone bust and started again before he was twenty-five. Carl Laemmle underwent a dozen changes of employment before becoming manager of a Wisconsin clothing store. Fox had a succession of jobs, always conducting ingenious money-making (and as often money-losing) schemes on the side, before starting his own 'shrinking and examining' business in the garment trade, an occupation that later led to his being characterized as a former 'pants presser' or 'pant sponger'. In these trades they usually did fairly well and accumulated sufficient modest capital to enter the amusement-arcade and nickelodeon business when the chance came. Perhaps they would have done spectacularly well had they remained in their original lines of business; after all the three friends who had emigrated from Germany with Carl Laemmle each made a fortune in the more mundane pursuits of manufacturing candy, furs and fancy goods. Anyway, none of the future tycoons was broke or a total failure and when their big opportunity did come they were well equipped: hardened to accept setbacks and come out fighting; in close touch with America's urban hordes who formed a microcosm of the mass world-wide audience; experienced in trades that were closely related to fashion and consequently at the mercy of changes in public taste. They understood the techniques of salesmanship and how to apply them brashly and without inhibition. Equally they had not too much to lose and no particular reason to regret abandoning their present undertakings: the thought that the film business might be only a temporary boom, soon to be replaced by some new craze in no way deterred them. In this respect the earliest figures – Laemmle, Loew, Fox, Zukor and Goldwyn – form an interesting group: in their late thirties, highly talented, experienced in business, full of confidence, and yet ready to embark on a wholly new activity of which they had little knowledge and which might prove of brief duration. They had been hanging around for just some such chance, and although the competition was harsh it did not come from those established interests that might have been attracted to the cinema. Their competitors were almost entirely adventurers, small scale entrepreneurs, men of little account like themselves. The legitimate theatre sneered at the cinema and orthodox financiers were not to be drawn. The wealthy bankers of New York – Jewish and gentile alike – were slow to assist the emergent industry; in fact the first banker to take the cinema seriously was the Californian A. P. Giannini, the son of an Italian immigrant, whose Bank of Italy (later re-named the Bank of America) has played an important part in movie finance since before the first world war. The bankers, the actors and the theatrical impresarios had first to be courted by the likes of Zukor and Loew. Later they jumped on the bandwagon of success. And having taken their seats the bankers sought a grip on the reins.

The strong Jewish representation among the founders of the film industry is, as we have seen, largely an accident of history rather than, as has often been suggested, a reflection of any easily definable Jewish traits. The same is true of the preponderance of Italians in the upper reaches of organized crime or the Irish in urban machine politics. As Seymour Martin Lipset observes in *The First New Nation*[1];

Since the emphasis is on individual success in the United States, those individuals or groups who feel themselves handicapped and who seek to resolve their consequent doubts about their personal worth are under strong pressure to 'innovate', that is, to use whatever means they can find to gain recognition. The pressure to innovate may be reflected in efforts which established groups would not make – for example, the development of new and risky industries by those of recent immigrant background and low status who are barred, by

[1]London, Heinemann, 1964, pp. 175-6.

limited economic resources and social discrimination, from advancing up economic ladders.

To their innovatory activites the budding tycoons brought a phenomenal capacity for hard work. 'For more than thirty years,' said William Fox, 'I avoided carrying a watch. I never wanted to know what time it was. My day ended when my day's work was completed. Again and again I did not go to bed at all during the twenty-four hours.' And to this capacity was added a complete ruthlessness engendered by their hard boyhoods, reinforced by their early struggles, compounded by the fight against the Trust, and necessary every day in their cut-throat world. This characteristic hardly set them apart from the Goulds, the Rocke-fellers, the Morgans, who had made their fortunes during the Gilded Age that followed the Civil War, with a creed defined by Mark Twain as: 'Get money. Get it quickly. Get it in abundance. Get it in prodigious abundance. Get it dishonestly if you can, honestly if you must.' In all fairness one must observe that the embryo movie tycoons were bent upon obtaining their money honestly, and for all their manifest double-dealing, connivance, back-stabbing and shoddy behaviour their careers are almost saintly in comparison with America's preceding age of entrepreneurs.

Another quality the early tycoons had is summed up in the Yiddish word *'chutzpah'* which is inadequately translated as 'cheek' and exemplified in the daily lives of all of them, and best perhaps in the accound of how Lewis J. Selznick got into the movies. In 1912 the Universal Company was in a state of chaos as Carl Laemmle and his Irish rival Pat Powers struggled for control. Selznick was a diamond salesman, and one day he happened to enter Universal's New York premises – depending upon which of many versions of the story one believes, he was there to hawk his wares or to offer an influential packet of shares to Laemmle under the cover of selling diamonds. Anyway, having made his entrance he rapidly concluded that the movies were a far more promising business than his present rather shaky occupation. He later observed that motion-picture production 'takes less brains than anything else in the world'. So taking advantage of the confusion, he picked himself a desk and confidently settled down to work, his position unchallenged as no one knew which of the several disputing factions had appointed him. Soon he had his name on a letterhead and was deeply involved in making pictures. In a short time, and in a manner that resembles some vicious Brechtian satire on the operation of big business, he had elevated himself to the position of general manager. Eventually when Laemmle emerged victorious in his battle with Powers and looked around through the settling dust to see who was in charge of the store, he discovered that it was the ex-diamond salesman. Selznick was rapidly fired, but by this time he had such a command of the business and so many contacts that he was able to set up on his own. That is *chutzpah*.

This buccaneering quality has been seen by many observers as *the* essential quality of the early moguls, though it did not always reveal itself in quite such an endearing way. Some had it in their youth and later played it down when they survived to become the industry's elder statesmen. One would never think in reading the memoirs of the benign octogenarian 'Mr Movies' Adolph Zukor that he had planted as many knives in the backs of his opponents as a full-strength Chinese tong in the busy season. One recipient of a carefully aimed Zukor blade was Lewis J. Selznick and it finished him. Jack L. Warner, however, was to demonstrate *chutzpah* in its pristine, amusing form, at the age of seventy when he bought the screen rights to *My Fair Lady* from the Columbia Broadcasting System for a record-breaking fee. CBS President William Paley failed to turn up for a photograph to publicize the deal, so Warner had his publicity department superimpose Paley's head on an earlier picture of Warner shaking hands with a diminutive official of Radio City Music Hall. After this fake appeared in the press there was an angry call objecting to the ruse and to the fact that Paley was made to appear shorter than Jack Warner. To which the tycoon's reply was: 'Call the CBS guy back and tell him that if a man had just handed me five and a half million I wouldn't care if he was ten inches taller.'

Now a man ten inches shorter than the dapper, moustachioed

Jack Warner would have found little difficulty in getting a job in a circus. Yet standing among his fellow tycoons Warner is by no means undersized. One could have swung a scythe five and a half feet off the ground at a gathering of movie moguls without endangering many lives; several would scarcely have heard the swish. The average height of the chief executives must have been somewhere in the region of five foot four or five inches. Above them soared William Fox and the bald dome of Samuel Goldwyn, though not to any great height; while most could have given a couple of inches to the gnome-like Carl Laemmle, who scarcely reached five foot two inches, and A. C. Blumenthal (a shady Los Angeles realtor who became one of the industry's most notorious backstage fixers and participant in the unseating of Fox), who was under five feet.

What exact effect their size had on them is difficult to say. Unquestionably they all evidenced the bouncy aggressiveness and drive traditionally associated with small men. As they were growing up and coming to power there was an upsurge of American interest in that hero of small men and megalomaniacs, Napoleon. A host of books appeared, Napoleon death-masks sold well in novelty stores, businessmen formed collections of Bonapartiana. William Randolph Hearst, whose newspapers cultivated the urban masses, had a painting of Napoleon behind his desk and went to fancy dress balls as the Little Corporal. The cult emphasized conquest, empire-building, the establishment of grandiose international systems, and glorified the achievements of a small uneducated foreigner of humble birth who rose to the heights through diligence, untutored genius and ruthless action. Such a cult undoubtedly had a great appeal for those who saw themselves in a similar position, and it is hardly surprising that over the past fifty years nearly every one of the diminutive tycoons should have been referred to in the press as a 'Napoleon', if sometimes with the addition of the semi-superfluous adjective 'little'. They were flattered by the comparison.

Despite the lack of inches the moguls were all pretty well built, solid chunky men for the most part, radiating an air of physical toughness that verged in some cases on the menacing. Their tempers were legendary, and no one's more so than that of the beefy Louis B. Mayer, who as a boy had joined salvage crews off the coast of Nova Scotia. Although he could also turn on the charm he was often vicious with his staff; on several occasions his post-second-world-war second in command, the sensitive Dore Schary, went outside to vomit after watching Mayer humiliate a subordinate. Mayer was genuinely violent. Once he knocked down Charlie Chaplin in a Los Angeles hotel after Charlie had made an allegedly offensive remark about his ex-wife Mildred Chaplin who was then working for Mayer. On another chivalrous occasion he struck Erich von Stroheim when the Austrian director offered the opinion that 'all women are whores'. Like most of his fellow tycoons, Mayer was deeply attached to his mother, and had an almost religious regard for motherhood; and if in his later years he was not above employing a man to work as his personal pimp, he would brook no base accusation against the generality of women. Fortunately there were several henchmen standing by to restrain Stroheim from retaliation. Even when well into his fifties and looking like a benevolent judge, Mayer would still grapple with visitors to his office when all else failed; on several occasions he had to be dragged off the recumbent form of some startled suppliant who had thought it unwise to offer more than token resistance to the most highly salaried executive in the United States. Even those who, unlike Mayer, had little taste for fisticuffs had needed the protection of strong-arm men in their early battle against the Trust. Looking back to the time when he worked in the New York police department and William Fox was fighting the Patent Company, the short, plump, blue-eyed Irishman Winfield Sheehan recalled: 'Anyway, about then Bill Fox needed a standing army and he came to me to raise it.' Soon Fox's New York office was bristling with brawny ex-cops; twenty years later, a reformed Sheehan was seeing his production of *Cavalcade* collect an Academy Award.

Despite a residual coarseness in language and conduct, there was no touch of the bohemian or even the *nouveau riche* about their dress, which is more than can be said for the ostentatious style in which they lived, their houses being smaller versions of the baroque cathedrals and palaces they erected for the delectation of those who patronized their films. All dressed with impeccable, conservative good taste. (Neckties were perhaps an exception.) Indeed clothes were something to which they attached great importance. Samuel Goldwyn, for instance, never carried money or anything else in his pockets in order to show off the cut of his suit to perfection – a single coin even might have disturbed his immaculate sartorial conception. Harry Cohn, during a visit to Europe in the 1930s, allegedly took the opportunity of a meeting with the Duke of Kent to secure the release of a special bolt of cloth from the Duke's Savile Row tailor. For some a sense of style derived from their experience in the garment trade; and a desire to appear well turned out is a reasonable characteristic of those bent on social acceptance. But beyond this there was an evident wish to create an atmosphere of solid, bourgeois respectability to win the confidence of bankers, public officials, opinion leaders, and to distinguish themselves from their often outlandishly attired employees.

10 Twenty years after the death of brother Sam in 1927, the surviving Warner Brothers, Jack, Harry and Albert, celebrate the anniversary of the coming of sound which made their company a major force in the industry.

11 (*Left*) Nicholas Schenck, drugstore and amusement park proprietor, who succeeded Marcus Loew as president of Loew's Inc. in 1927 and remained at the top until 1955. As a senior aide once remarked of M-G-M movies: 'What Mr Schenck is in favour of we are for. All of us here like pictures that do well at the box-office'. 12 (*right*) Harry Cohn, creator, with his elder brother Jack, of Columbia films and the only person to be both president and head of production of a major movie company. Perhaps no other Hollywood tycoon has excited such violent and various responses from his peers and employees as 'King Cohn'.

13 David Wark Griffith with Joseph M. Schenck (right), brother of Nicholas, and as an independent producer, chairman of United Artists and co-founder of 20th Century-Fox one of the most influential figures in Hollywood history.

EAST COAST, WEST COAST

> When you make a steel rail you make something
> that is so long and so heavy and of such a
> quality. But when you make a foot of film, it
> is subject to the judgment of millions of people,
> each with his own standard of measurement.
> Joseph P. Kennedy

The founders of the major studios had little prior knowledge of show business. Carl Laemmle had carried a spear for a couple of nights when Edwin Booth visited Chicago with *Julius Caesar* in the 1880s and William Fox was briefly a member of a spare-time juvenile song-and-dance act called, it is said, the Smaltz Brothers. Those born after 1890 had a little more experience: Sam Katz played the piano in a Laemmle cinema, the eleven-year-old Jack Warner sang as a boy soprano between reels when the Warner brothers first toured Ohio showing movies; Harry Cohn spent several years as a Tin Pan Alley song-plugger and was briefly accompanied at the piano as a vaudeville act by one Harry Rubenstein who was subsequently to gain fame as half of the Kalmar and Ruby song-writing team, the authors of many hit numbers such as 'Nevertheless' and 'Three Little Words'. The only major exceptions were Samuel Goldwyn's first partners, the cornet-playing impresario Jesse Lasky and the out-of-work actor Cecil B. DeMille, and Zukor's creative collaborator in Famous Players, Edwin S. Porter. Porter, who directed the pace-setting *Great Train Robbery* of 1903, retired from the business in 1915 with his share of Famous Players' money, most of which he later lost in the Wall Street crash; DeMille ran his own company during the 1920s and then spent the rest of his life as an employee, albeit a most respected one and with his own unit, of Paramount films. Both Porter and DeMille had been the second choices of Goldwyn and Zukor, each of whom had been turned down by the great D. W. Griffith, whose star was to wax as his rejected collaborators rose, and wane while they remained firmly at the top.

Yet while most lacked serious creative talent, nearly all of them had an indefinable flair that expressed itself in their skill at handling publicity and show business packaging, and in the astuteness with which they discovered and shaped talent. Nowhere is this seen more clearly than in the Star System that derived in the first instance from the moguls' fight against the Trust. As the Star System rapidly became one of the (if not *the*) principal economic and artistic cornerstones of the business, and as it was the tycoons' task to decide on which performers to put under contract and exploit, the continuing ability to take the right decisions was perhaps the most important creative function the moguls had. And the majority of them evidenced over the years this talent-spotting gift in a remarkable degree. Louis B. Mayer, for instance, immediately saw in the young Greta Garbo – before she spoke a word of English – the star quality that only later became apparent to others, as well as superintending the way that she should be employed at M-G-M. On a single trip to Europe in the 'thirties he signed up Greer Garson, after being impressed by her on the London stage, as well as Hedy Lamarr. Others, such as Harry Cohn, who had little major talent under contract in his early days, saw new ways of exploiting or combining various performers. Occasionally, as with Samuel Goldwyn, another major star-maker, they might be so blind to the possibilities of failure that they would persist in attempting to put a performer over as a 'star' when it was long clear that the public had no intention of accepting him or her. Goldwyn's big fiasco was the Russian actress, Anna Sten, who never learned to speak English with any degree of feeling, despite endless lessons; Goldwyn persisted, at vast expense in wasted weeks of shooting and poor box-office returns, in his conviction that Miss Sten could be a major star, before reluctantly admitting defeat. Of course, as one looks back through fading trade journals and fan magazines, one appreciates what a large percentage of the moguls' swans turned out to be geese, and how short the careers of most performers proved to be. There has always been something strangely unreal and fantastic about the whole Star System anyway, as that expert on the essential ludicrousness of the movie business, Lewis J. Selznick, once testified. Questioned by a reporter in the early 'twenties as to why he didn't advertise his pictures on street-cars, where most of his potential audience would see the ads, Selznick replied:

It is a waste of money. My stars don't ride on street-cars. They have their own motor cars and would never see this advertising. There is no use putting advertising where the stars won't see it. The magazines and billboards they see, with their names in big type, and it keeps them happy and contented.

As the industry settled down into a marked division between the West and East Coasts the ex-furriers and former glove-salesmen had to decide on which side of the business they belonged: supervising production in Hollywood or handling distribution, publicity and finance in New York. The more extrovert, more colourful figures – those for whom the accent in 'show business' fell on the 'show' – tended to gravitate towards Hollywood. Sometimes the split happened in families. Jack and Sam Warner were moviemakers and ran the California studio; Harry and Albert were businessmen and sat in the head office in New York. The sharp, wise-cracking Jack Warner once wrote of his stolid brother Harry that 'he never cut a foot of film anywhere', and of the cool Albert, 'To him celluloid was something they use to make combs and brushes'. The smooth, calculating Nick Schenck succeeded his mentor Marcus Loew as head of Loew's Inc. in New York, while his brother, the fast-living, fun-loving showman Joe Schenck was a Hollywood figure. The beefy, aggressive Harry Cohn, who uniquely was both president and head of production at Columbia, spent most of his life in Hollywood in constant conflict with his elder brother Jack, a gentler, frailer, bespectacled figure who ran the business end in New York. When Harry visited the company's headquarters or Jack came to the West Coast, neither would speak officially to the other without witnesses present. Nor was there much love lost between Nicholas Schenck and his so-called employee, the M-G-M production chief Louis Mayer; Mayer in private pronounced

Schenck's name 'skunk' and claimed that 'I've got more brains in my ass than Mr Skunk has in his head'.[1]

Adolph Zukor was also a New York man though in 1937, in his mid-sixties, he went out to Hollywood and spent a year personally superintending several productions during Paramount's economic recovery and into his nineties was making annual trips out West. While never entirely the accountant that the majority of New York people were, he had little knowledge of movie-making: 'I was secretly envious,' he once wrote, 'of those who had an intimate hand in production and making myself inconspicuous often watched activities.' Nevertheless he was, at the height of his career, more concerned with the acquisition of cinemas than with the individual manufacture of films: the opening in 1926 of the magnificent Paramount Theatre in New York, a tangible monument to his success, was clearly a more significant achievement in his eyes than any single film screened there, for the obvious reason that it was more his own work. Zukor actually said at the dinner to celebrate the Paramount's opening: 'I do not think that this is any monument to me, as you gentleman have suggested, but rather a monument dedicated to America, to think that a country could give a chance to a boy like me to be connected with an institution like this.' And for his close friend Marcus Loew films were always so many job lots to be sold by the dubious and later illegal system of block-booking. Some figures who were only concerned with the exhibition of films remained outside the industry altogether, like the great New York movie impresario Samuel 'Roxy' Rothafel and his Californian counterpart Sid Grauman, creator of Grauman's Chinese Theatre, the Hollywood Boulevard cinema where the filmstars left their footprints (or in the case of dogs and horses, their paw and hoof marks) in cement.

In 1928 Sidney Kent told the National Conference on Motion Pictures: 'This business is a form of art. It has to have a combin-

[1]For the record, the rough pronunciation of Schenck is 'Skenk', Laemmle is 'Lemlee', Schary is 'Sharree', Goetz is 'Gets', Wanger is 'Wainjer', Loew is 'Low', while for business purposes Cecil B. DeMille sported a capital 'D' and used the modest small 'd' for private life, the pronunciation being much the same in both usages.

ation of pictures that we know will be successful at the box-office, and of "prestige" pictures that are made to push the industry ahead.' The studio bosses were caught between these two pressures: from New York the demand was for a steady supply of easily saleable movies made at the lowest possible cost, while in Hollywood the more ambitious writers and directors wanted to make individual movies of quality that would 'push the industry ahead'. The result was an uneasy compromise that inevitably favoured the New York viewpoint. As early as 1920, in a dispute over scripts, DeMille wrote from Hollywood to the Famous Players-Lasky head office that 'while there is no question in anyone's mind that the New York office is the seat of government, there is considerable doubt in our minds that it is the seat of great literary and dramatic discernment'; few artists were later in a position to send such direct missives. The chain of command from New York through the studio bosses and their executive producers meant that the people who actually made the pictures were rarely able to confront those who had the final decision on their work. Yet the very remoteness of Hollywood from the company headquarters had the effect in prosperous years of reducing some of the pressure that greater proximity would have brought. The usual form of travel between the coasts was a three-day train journey; not until after the second world war did it become customary to fly except in cases of direst emergency.

Ironically, and very significantly, the 1950s break-up of the studio system by independent production and the consequent artistic freedom that resulted (especially where this involved overseas or location shooting) was managed from New York and not Hollywood, for it was to the head office that the independents went for finance. The ramifications of the situation are highly complicated and one might observe in passing the situation of Budd Schulberg. *On the Waterfront* (1954) was a Sam Spiegel production for Columbia, made on location in Hoboken, New York; Schulberg won one of the film's seven Academy Awards for his original screenplay. Jack Cohn was involved in the decision to back it. A year later Columbia attempted to persuade Schulberg to adapt for the cinema his prize-fight novel *The Harder They*

Fall, which the company had acquired for Hollywood production. Schulberg refused on the grounds that because Harry Cohn had deliberately humiliated his father, Ben Schulberg, during his period of decline when he superintended Columbia's 'B' movies, he would never set foot in Columbia's California studio.

To characterize the men who ran the studios as merely businessmen would be misleading. Few of the studios were run in a way that approximated to any standard notion of business efficiency; their administration and accountancy were quite unlike those of large corporations. Louis B. Mayer, for thirty years the head of Hollywood's largest studio, was described by an associate as 'the worst manager I have met in all my life' – which did not necessarily mean he was unsuited to the job. Given the flushness of the times a great deal of money could be squandered without anyone worrying unduly. Only for B-features and run-of-the-mill material was it important to break even or make a small profit; for big feature films vast profits were sought and a large loss could be borne with equanimity. When the West Coast offices were seized by desires for economy and put in solid businessmen to run production, the results were usually disastrous, as proved the case at Paramount in the early 'thirties when Jesse Lasky and Ben Schulberg were replaced by taxi-cab tycoons and accountants. Rarely of course did the moguls ever stint in rewarding themselves. In any comparative industrial listing of the percentage of net profits or total expenditure that went to executive remuneration, the movies always came high on the list, usually second. A great deal of time at shareholders' meetings was taken up questioning the sums paid to executives; the protests were invariably made in vain. Even when at times of crisis the studio bosses took cuts in salaries, these always proved, upon examination, to have been illusory.

Moviemaking, so the old moguls felt and no doubt justly, was *sui generis* neither an art nor a business. This did not prevent them from claiming it was a business when charged with its failure as art, or that it was an art when charged with its failure as business. J. B. Priestley acutely put his finger on the contradiction after a visit to Hollywood some thirty years ago :

Its trade, which is in dreams at so many dollars per thousand feet, is managed by businessmen pretending to be artists and by artists pretending to be businessmen. In this queer atmosphere, nobody stays as he was; the artist begins to lose his art, and the businessman becomes temperamental and overbalanced.[2]

This tug is seen in the word 'studio' itself. In the early days movies were made in 'factories'; then the moguls introduced the more high-sounding term 'studio' for the place of production and 'laboratory' for the processing departments. As the 'Trust' boss Jeremiah Kennedy remarked when bringing the latter name to Biograph sixty years ago: 'We can get a better type of people to work in a laboratory. It sounds like something and a film plant ought to be a laboratory anyway.' Likewise the moguls preferred 'motion pictures' to movies, flickers or any other early term; and it was Louis Mayer who gave the Academy of Motion Picture Arts and Sciences its name.

Yet the studios *were* factories of a kind and they had to be. Edwin S. Porter had appreciated the situation back in 1914 when Famous Players were faced with the prospect of having to deliver a film a week to their distributors. 'There's not enough picture talent in the world to make that many pictures in a year,' he said. But that and many more had to be produced, and so the studios had to be organized on a factory belt system. To attend on the muse was not enough. Yet this kind of mass production was not, as Joseph Kennedy rightly observed, like making steel rails. However much films copy from each other, run in series

[2]*Midnight on the Desert* (London, Heinemann, 1937), p. 193. The Hollywood section in this 'Chapter of Autobiography' is a characteristically vivid and searching account of the movie colony in the 'thirties. It is highly critical but very fair. Of the moguls, Priestley observes:

'Rich men in the film industry are often ignorant and stupid and have far too much power, but then rich men in many other industries are often ignorant and stupid and have far too much power. That familiar criticism is really one of the capitalist system, not specially of Hollywood. We can see that in films the man who controls the purse does not necessarily make a good leader. But why only in films? Perhaps I had heard too many of these funny stories, but certainly I had always been surprised by the quick intelligence of most of the people I had met in Hollywood. They were not quite the tremendous fellows they obviously thought they were, but they were not the ignorant buffoons and mountebanks they are often reported to be.'

and cycles, supporting Dorothy Parker's dictum that the only 'ism' Hollywood believes in is plagiarism, each one is something of an individual item.

Everybody inveighed against this system. 'The movies will never be worth a hoot,' wrote George Jean Nathan in 1928, 'until the business end of the enterprise is absolutely and entirely separated from the actual producing department, and until nine-tenths of those presently in control of the latter are fired.'[3] Such a demand on a commercial undertaking is impossible, which is not to say that no moguls cared about making better movies nor that from time to time they did not allow their employees a moderate and often even complete freedom. Naturally anyone whose films consistently made a profit was left alone; and those who were content to interpret exactly the requirements of their bosses had little trouble. Others fought a running battle over the years, winning occasional small victories and, when the moguls' backs were turned, sometimes large ones. There are no general principles to be deduced from this. Very definitely one can say that artists enjoyed their greatest liberty between *Birth of a Nation* in 1915 and the formation in 1924 of M-G-M, the company associated with the development of 'strong' production. 'When banks came into pictures, trouble came with them,' said Cecil B. De-Mille. 'When we operated on picture money, there was joy in the industry, when we operated on Wall Street money, there was grief in the industry.' These Golden Years of early Chaplin, of Griffith, of Mack Sennett's Keystone comedies, of Keaton, passed with the arrival of the big studio system. Yet the situation was never completely rigid thereafter. In 1918 Erich von Stroheim had been given the go-ahead by Carl Laemmle to make his first picture *Blind Husbands* on the basis of no reputation and a mere outline on a sheet of paper; subsequently he fell victim to increasing interference and eventual exclusion. (Laemmle's only real interference came over the title, which Stroheim intended to be *The Pinnacle*. 'What means this word *pinnacle*?' the tycoon allegedly asked. 'The public won't know what it is about. There

[3] *Art of the Night* (New York/London, Alfred A. Knopf, 1928), p. 110.

are more blind husbands about than there are pinnacles, so we'll call it *Blind Husbands*.') But in 1941 another tyro, Orson Welles, was given total latitude by RKO to make *Citizen Kane* on the strength of his radio and stage work; then he had all but one of his subsequent Hollywood pictures tampered with (*Macbeth* at Republic is the one exception), though not always unreasonably. Subsequently both Welles and Stroheim were to be more welcome as actors than as directors. The dictatorial Harry Cohn, however, gave Frank Capra a completely free hand and was often only able to secure the services of certain directors by agreeing not even to speak with them in the course of shooting. Similarly Louis B. Mayer was prepared to let a producer or director go ahead on a project to teach him a lesson, in the hope that he would fall on his face. Mayer once told an aspirant director whom he preferred to continue employing as a producer that a man must learn to crawl before he can walk; he also believed evidently that a man who had fallen on his face would be happier to crawl in the future. Generally no one in what was essentially a producer's cinema could claim to be wholly free and unhampered on more than the occasional project. Genuinely outsize talents and awkward non-conformists found life difficult in Hollywood. And no one's work or reputation was sacrosanct in the eyes of the bosses. Whether true or not, Jack Warner claims: 'I have had a hand in the editing of every picture ever made by Warner Brothers.' The studio heads were not merely the ultimate but the immediate and inter-mediate arbiters: indeed, as the old Hollywood joke has it, they were 'czars of all the rushes'. D. W. Griffith had seen it coming with the M-G-M merger in 1924: 'Rex, you and I are building on sand,' he said to fellow director Rex Ingram. And a few got out, including Ingram who for a while made films, financed by Marcus Loew, in the south of France.

The trouble with most of the moguls was that they thought they knew about everything – from business and public taste to script-writing and direction. In their board-room eyries, sur-rounded by yes-men to boost their confidence, living in a self-contained community set apart even from local Los Angeles society (which initially looked down on movie folk), they grew ever further away from the lives of normal people and were not forced to pay heed to the opinions of their underlings. When Mayer, the self-styled expert on the behaviour of the American family, re-wrote the scripts of the Andy Hardy series, there was nobody to challenge him; they were after all playing the game with his football. Or take the case of Buster Keaton. When he was forced to leave independent production, being almost sold in fact by his brother-in-law, Joseph Schenck, to Joe's brother Nick Schenck at M-G-M, he ran into his first real conflict with producers. And if M-G-M cannot carry all the blame for Keaton's decline, he himself knew that troubles lay ahead from the moment the producer (Irving Thalberg's brother-in-law Lawrence Weingarten) assigned to his second M-G-M movie *Spite Marriage* (1929) viewed the rushes and said: 'Don't bother to tear that sequence down. I don't like that type of thing in *my* pictures.'

There were many ways of running a studio, many styles of co-ordinating the activities of the hundreds of stars, directors, writers and technicians that each company had under contract. The two extremes are represented by men very conscious of their personal image: the vague, quixotic Carl Laemmle, who wanted to be loved, and the harsh, brutal Harry Cohn, who wanted to be feared.

Although capable of great tenacity in business negotiations, the quiet little Laemmle was known to his employees with genuine affection as 'Uncle Carl', and after the birth of his first grandchild in 1930 as 'Grandpa Carl'. This public persona had been shaped by the man once described as 'the father of cinema publicity', the former Ohio newspaperman Robert Cochrane, publicity adviser during Laemmle's fight against the Trust and later vice-president at Universal. When Laemmle was absent from the studios, as he often was in the 1920s, he left others in charge, occasionally with a rather undefined authority, and there was a genuine sense of warmth and loyalty felt towards him by his staff. The tall, brawny Harry Cohn, on the other hand, developed a deliberately rebarbative manner, delighted in humiliating his employees, estranged many of his best artists, and was dubbed 'White Fang' by Ben Hecht. 'I don't have ulcers. I give them,' he once boasted. The director Charles Vidor unsuccessfully attempted to break his Columbia contract on the grounds of Cohn's notoriously foul language; Cohn had sound stages wired so that he could listen to employees' private conversations; at one Christmas party in his studio he put a secretary in his swivel chair and invited her to point to anyone in the room – and Cohn would fire him as a Christmas present to her. Like many another mogul such as Louis Mayer, Cohn used his power to satisfy his formidable sexual appetite; from his office ran a secret corridor to the dressing room reserved for selected contract starlets. Like others too he could wreak terrible vengeance on those who crossed him. But, unlike Mayer, he seldom pursued the relentless vendettas that were such a part of Hollywood life. Cohn was capable, however, of having an elaborate electric chair installed in the company's executive dining room. Uneasy newcomers would be steered into this seat and from a button on the floor the president himself would administer a painful shock to the hapless occupant. In a less sadistic form this passion for practical jokes was shared by many of his peers.

The fortunes of Universal, sad to relate, gradually declined under Laemmle while those of Columbia steadily rose under Cohn in both quality and annual profits. This is not to say that Cohn's approach was necessary to get results, and generally the behaviour of the studio bosses fell somewhere between these two extremes. The paternalism of Laemmle and the dictatorship of Cohn both led to the same conclusion – that anything to do with the studio or anyone connected with it became the moguls' business. For instance, and typically, when in 1932 the M-G-M producer Paul Bern (middle-aged husband of the studio's blonde star, Jean Harlow) committed suicide, the company's own police and Louis B. Mayer were called to the scene long before the Los Angeles homicide squad. And it was only with difficulty that the M-G-M publicity chief managed to persuade Mayer to hand over to the official investigator the famous suicide note which he had pocketed. When in the mid-fifties there were rumours circulating concerning the possibility of a marriage between Sammy Davis Jr and Columbia's top contract star, Kim Novak, Harry

Cohn is said to have immediately put the heat on the black entertainer through his underworld network. Unless the association was broken off, Davis was threatened with losing most of his future night club work across America. Davis's engagement to a coloured singer was announced shortly afterwards; in the course of the intrigue the worried Cohn experienced a near fatal heart attack.

As to why anyone put up with working for someone remotely like Harry Cohn or Louis B. Mayer, the answer is that the pay was good and you either worked for them or went into some other business. Actually, it is not quite as simple as that for it must be said that however outrageous the moguls were, a good many sensitive, intelligent artists managed to get along with them – often with difficulty perhaps, but usually quite well. Some even found a congenial side to them, or were fascinated by their barbarousness; some managed to get by with no more than occasional contact. William Faulkner for instance obtained Jack Warner's permission to work at home instead of at the studio, and it was only when Warner tried to call Faulkner's Hollywood apartment that he discovered that 'home' meant Oxford, Mississippi.[4] Nor was the moguls' judgment always as absurd as it is sometimes made out to be. It is not logical to attribute to them total power and at the same time deny them any credit for the good films that emerged from their studios.

The frequently appalling behaviour of these men can be attributed in part to their insecurity – to a well-founded fear that plots were afoot in New York and around the studios to unseat them and that their more artistically gifted underlings were sneering at them behind their backs. Year after year they saw colleagues toppled overnight from their positions of power. Having con-

[4]This celebrated Hollywood story is almost certainly true. I put it in this form because Jack Warner chooses to tell it against himself in his autobiography; the screenwriter George Oppenheimer observes in his own memoirs that 'At Warners all writers were required by the autocratic Jack Warner to be clocked in at nine and stay until five'. However, Faulkner did not work at Warners until the 1940s, and in a most interesting article on 'Faulkner in Hollywood' (*Man and the Movies* ed. W. R. Robinson, Louisiana State University Press, 1967), Joseph Blotner dates the story from the early 'thirties when Faulkner was employed by M-G-M.

spired with others to depose rivals, they were ever on the out-
look for similar conspiracies directed against themselves. No one
trusted anyone else and with good reason. William Fox, the classic over-reacher, attempted to buy simultaneously the Gaumont-
British cinema chain in Britain and Loew's Inc., and Nicholas
Schenck was prepared to sell without informing Louis Mayer in
Hollywood. Mayer's influence in Washington – through his friend
President Hoover – helped to avert the bid, and Fox's chief lieutenant Winfield Sheehan joined in the final bankers' push that
edged Fox into oblivion. By 1936 Fox was bankrupt, and five
years later he was convicted of bribing the judge who heard his
bankruptcy case and sent to gaol for a year. Carl Laemmle was
forced out of Universal three years before his death, and Mayer
was eventually given no choice but to resign from M-G-M.
During the 'thirties the top management at RKO and Paramount
changed yearly. In such an unpredictable business no one knew
who would go next, or when the magic 'touch' would desert them
– even if they knew exactly what this 'touch' consisted of. To
say that William Fox ('I always bragged of the fact that no second
of those contained in the twenty-four hours ever passed but that
the name of William Fox was on the screen, being exhibited in
some theatre in some part of the world') might have suffered from
megalomania or that Harry Cohn's conduct evidenced certain
symptoms of clinical paranoia is only saying that Fox's ambitions
and Cohn's insecurity took a somewhat more extreme form than
others in a community torn by ruthless ambition and riddled with
insecurity.

A wild inconsistency of conduct was the norm among studio
heads: they came raving on to the sets to settle problems, alter-
nately raging at their employees or getting down on their knees to
them. Reason and reserve were at a premium in Hollywood. The
stabler personalities tended to be in New York and they were not
liked by their more histrionic West Coast colleagues. One of
these New York men, as I mentioned a few pages back, was
Adolph Zukor, the Mikoyan of Paramount who managed to sur-
vive every shake-up over a period of fifty years to become chairman emeritus in his nineties. Zukor was a quiet, chilly, calculating

character, known behind his back as 'Creepy'. Few were permitted to address him by his first name: nearly forty years passed before Zukor and Jesse Lasky were on Christian name terms; DeMille worked with and under him for four decades and never called him anything but 'Mr Zukor'. When DeMille broke with Zukor in 1923 to go off for a while on his own he was told, after an association of nearly ten years, 'Cecil, you have never been one of us'. The impetuosity, the reliance upon hunches, the snap decisions of his contemporaries were not for him. Zukor would take long nocturnal walks through New York that in the course of a night would lead him down town to the Battery and up to Central Park again. At the end of such peripatetic cogitations he would have arrived at a decision and calculated the necessary strategy to realize his aim, which he would then pursue with complete ruthlessness. It was after such walks that he proceeded to unseat the head of the Paramount distributing company and install his own nominee (and a little later himself), and to issue the ultimatum that drove Samuel Goldwyn out of Famous Players-Lasky. ('Mr Lasky,' Zukor is reported as saying to his vice-president about the company's chairman, 'I'm sorry to tell you but Famous Players-Lasky is not large enough to hold Mr Goldwyn and myself. You brought him into the company and I don't want to ask him to leave. But you'll have to choose between Mr Goldwyn and me. I'm going to the country for the weekend, and I'll await your decision there.' Said Goldwyn with some understatement, 'I don't think it was a nice thing for him to do.') This studied remoteness coupled with a sharp wit, his age and reputation for probity (a relative affair in the movie business and one partly compounded by longevity) led to his becoming the elder statesman of the industry when other survivors of the earlier years qualified only as buffoons or social embarrassments. Zukor would not have told an interviewer, as Harry Cohn once did, that moviemaking was 'better than being a pimp'. Cohn was carefully kept away from the press by his own public relations staff who saw this as among their major tasks.

Few of the early pioneers survived as independent producers

outside the major studio framework. The only one to do so in a big way was Samuel Goldwyn, without question the most striking personality of them all. While the others fought to remain within the complex system they had created, Goldwyn's career after his departure from the company that bore his name was an investment in his own producing talent. He personally financed and carefully supervised every aspect of his own productions which he kept to a manageable number. He owned his own studio and released his pictures through United Artists or RKO, had his own stars under contract (to use himself or hire out with due acknowledgement), and borrowed others that he needed. His total belief in his own abilities was not entirely misplaced, as his record testifies, and his vanity knew no bounds. The Goldwyn publicity department as a matter of course hired parties of cameramen to bolster the crowd when he arrived in New York or Hollywood and laid on extras to fill press conferences to capacity. His advertising chief once put on his desk a draft for the poster to announce the forthcoming presentation of *We Live Again*, which read: 'The directorial genius of Mamoulian, the beauty of Sten and the producing genius of Goldwyn have been combined to make the world's greatest entertainment.' The boss glanced it over with an approving eye: 'That's the kind of ad I like. Facts. No exaggeration.' The outsize Goldwyn ego made it essential that he should be his own boss, as the history of his attempts to work with Adolph Zukor and the Selwyn brothers makes only too abundantly clear. Zukor allegedly told the Selwyn brothers: 'Sam is like a Jersey cow that gives the finest milk but before you can take the bucket away he has kicked it over.' Looking back on their brief association from a distance of forty years, Zukor revealingly commented:

Sam was not a believer, one might say, in parliamentary procedure. A chairman of the board does not ordinarily concern himself with the day to day details of operation. Sam did, and by temperament he had to go.

Unlike most of his contemporaries, Goldwyn became a public personality, one of the characters of his age. Perhaps, however, not quite to the extent he himself imagined. When in 1936 he heard that Alva Johnston was writing his biography he threatened to sue the *Saturday Evening Post,* in which the book was being serialized, and the publishers, Random House, if he found the slightest inaccuracy. When the book appeared it delighted Goldwyn so much that he distributed hundreds of copies to his friends. However, Goldwyn's fame – like that of all picture producers and directors – was more or less limited to New York and Hollywood. Citizens at large seemed only to care about the stars themselves. Countless book-sellers in the South and Middle West asked the salesmen, 'Who *is* this Great Goldwyn anyhow?' When this fact was reported to Goldwyn, he thought they were kidding him.

To his regret his films are less well remembered than his Goldwynisms, that remarkable series of immigrant's adventures with the English language, part mixed metaphor, part malapropism, part illiteracy, that have a power and pungency of their own. He was certainly responsible for the memorable phrase 'include me out', as well as 'the trouble with this business is the dearth of bad pictures', and 'they're always biting the hand that lays the golden egg'. A good many, however, were the inventions of Hollywood wits: his resident team of writers once coined a Goldwynism each, the first of which to appear in print attributed to their employer would bring its creator the jackpot – George Oppenheimer won with 'It rolls off my back like a duck'. Unfortunately the Goldwynisms have tended to present their creator as a clown instead of an extremely shrewd businessman and a constant force for improvement in the Hollywood cinema. This even Goldwyn's leading detractors (and many people have emerged wounded from encounters with him) have never denied. Certainly every film he made was a 'Goldwyn picture'.

The peculiar combination of caution and innovation in Goldwyn's films seems to reflect the limitations of his generation's tastes. He rarely made a picture from an original screenplay; instead he acquired literary or theatrical properties of proven quality which he proceeded to adapt with considerable fidelity.

14 and 15 A great Hollywood occasion: the official dedication and
designation as a state historical landmark in 1956 of the old barn on Jacob
Stern's farm in Hollywood village where Cecil B. DeMille had directed *The
Squaw Man* in 1913. The barn was shifted to Paramount's lot in 1927.
(*Above*) Jesse Lasky shakes hands with DeMille, with to left and right,
Samuel Goldwyn and Adolph Zukor enjoying their own private flashbacks.
(*Below*) DeMille expatiates in his best lay preacher's manner, attended by
Y. Frank Freeman (Vice-president of Paramount), Goldwyn and Lasky
(on left).

16 The ageing chairman of the Paramount board Adolph Zukor, with the ever-youthful star and tallest man on the Paramount lot, Gary Cooper.

17 Sam Katz, the immigrant barber's son who became a movie-house tycoon as a teenager, showing off M-G-M's Hungarian-born musical star Ilona Massey in the late thirties when he was in charge of musicals at M-G-M.

18 Walt Disney (right) takes the stage, at a 1962 presentation of awards by the Screen Producers Guild, with the former Greek shepherd boy Spyros Skouras, whose twenty-year occupancy of the 20th Century-Fox presidency was shortly to be terminated.

Some of this caution resulted from his experiences in the early 'twenties when he had been bowled over by literary names and brought many of them to Hollywood to produce original work. Few of them did. His encounter with Maeterlinck was especially disastrous, though the story that Goldwyn rushed out from reading Maeterlinck's first screenplay screaming: 'My God! The hero's a bee!' is certainly apocryphal. Not apocryphal is George Bernard Shaw's quip when he refused to sell Goldwyn the screen rights to his plays: 'The trouble, Mr Goldwyn, is that you are only interested in art and I am only interested in money.' One should not perhaps conclude from this remark that Shaw saw through the Hollywood set-up: he became fascinated (or hypnotized) by that weird Hungarian mini-tycoon Gabriel Pascal, to whom he entrusted, with far from satisfactory results, the cinematic exploitation of his works.[5]

Goldwyn of course, like all the moguls, was by no means indifferent to money. Yet he did believe in some indefinable notion of class and quality. 'Pictures built upon the strong foundation of art and refinement,' was how he was defining this idea in advertisements as early as 1916. Such beliefs were generally shared, or at least professed, in Hollywood, despite the widespread anti-intellectualism. Jack Warner, for instance, who has little reason to be ashamed of the steady stream of good films that came from his studio, has written that 'I would rather take a fifty-mile hike than crawl through a book. I prefer to skip the long ones and get a synopsis from the story department.' Once the director Mervyn LeRoy cabled Warner suggesting that he read Harvey Allen's *Anthony Adverse* and received the reply: 'Read it? I can't even lift it.' (But he did buy the novel, in the Hollywood sense of 'buy' and LeRoy filmed it for Warner Brothers.) Goldwyn was far too impatient to sit down and read a novel; he is said to have taken several days to get through *The Wizard of Oz* and once remarked of a book that 'I read part of it all the way through'. To the suggestion that his daughters might study at the university, an

[5]'We Go See Old Man', S. N. Behrman's amusing account of the Shaw-Pascal association is to be found in Behrman's *The Suspended Drawing Room* (London, Hamish Hamilton, 1966).

angry Louis Mayer exploded: 'A daughter of mine go to college? Become an *intellectual?*' Yet this aggressive tone, unattractive as it is, often revealed the wariness of sensitive, intelligent men aware of their lack of education, frightened of being taken in by phonies; and there were plenty of phonies around. Stories of their ignorance and philistinism are legion and legendary, but so too are they about Harold Ross, founder of the *New Yorker*. Yet most of them had aspirations to produce some works of artistic and social value along with the quantities of rubbish that kept the machine grinding.

Sadly, few of them developed any interests outside the cinema that would have widened their view of life. They did not read much, had little interest in the arts. 'We've got to be out of this joint in twenty minutes,' said Darryl Zanuck on a visit to the Louvre. In an official capacity they necessarily came into contact with people in public life and they travelled a great deal, on a mixture of pleasure and business. But absorbed in their work and socially insecure, they found the majority of their friends and acquaintances in their own small world. They dabbled in golf, hired people to buy works of art (Mayer had an imposing collection of Grandma Moses' paintings), and some developed odd obsessions, like Harry Cohn's for the law. But for most the only important leisure activity was gambling, a passion that survived from their youth and which they pursued with almost religious fervour. All of them played cards for large sums and threw dice. Even playing golf, William Fox was unable to savour the game without matching the number of the hole with a dollar bet, despite the fact that as a result of a boyhood accident in which he fell off a truck his left arm was paralysed and he played a one-armed game; while on his way to the links to compete against Nick Schenck in 1929 Fox was involved in the car accident that proved near-fatal personally, and, by putting him out of action for several vital weeks, turned out to be entirely fatal professionally. But it was horses that occupied the greatest amount of their spare time and energy: owning them, visiting the race tracks, and placing illegal off-track bets from the studio when they could not get away. Mayer became such a fanatical horse-breeder and racer that in the end a reluctant Nicholas Schenck (like his brother Joe a dedicated horse-player) had to force him to sell the stable. To Mayer's chagrin, his prize steeds went to Harry Warner. Likewise the gambling of Harry Cohn became so obsessive and widely publicized that his brother Jack had to warn him to slow down because of dangerous rumblings among company stockholders. Cohn was known to place bets of between five and ten thousand dollars daily, and is reputed to have lost as much as 400,000 dollars in one season.

Their gambling brought them into contact with an underworld of criminals and bookmakers, whose company they enjoyed, and with the international set of casino-goers and stable owners to whose company they aspired. There are many theories about the attraction of gambling. Beyond the more obvious ones, the Jewish novelist Chaim Bermant has interestingly examined it as a specifically Jewish phenomenon in an essay called *The Jewish Disease*.[6] 'Gambling is to the Jew what drink is to the Irishman', he says, though he points out that it is condemned by the *Mishnah* and the *Torah*. After canvassing several possible theories, and having traced the passion back beyond the ghetto and probably the Jewish exile too, Bermant concludes that, if there *is* any one explanation,

It may, and I think this may be the most likely cause, be due to Jewish optimism, the unpronounced conviction that God is there, hovering over the dice, loading the odds in one's favour. The belief in Jewish luck may be totally without foundation, but it is ineradicable from the Jewish breast.

F. Scott Fitzgerald, an Irish-American drawn to the bottle rather than to the gaming table, offered a fanciful explanation for the tycoons' interest in horses in *The Last Tycoon* when Monroe Stahr 'guessed that the Jews had taken over the worship of horses as a symbol – for years it had been the cossacks mounted and the Jews afoot. Now the Jews had horses and it gave them a sense of well-being and power.' The fiddler, as it were, came down off the roof and got into the saddle.

[6]*Quest* 2 (London, Cornmarket Press, 1967), pp. 66-7.

5

THE BOY WONDERS

The producer must be a prophet and a general, a
diplomat and a peacemaker, a miser and a spendthrift.
He must have vision tempered by hindsight, daring
governed by caution, the patience of a saint and the
iron will of a Cromwell. His decisions must be sure,
swift and immediate, as well as subject to change,
because conditions change continuously in the motion
picture industry. The producer's resources must be
such that no contingency can stop him finding a star,
soothing a director like a super-Talleyrand, or,
in all-night conference in shirt sleeves and heavy
cigar smoke, doctoring the scripts by his own creative
power.

Jesse L. Lasky

To their corporate ranks the former furriers, boilermakers,
glove salesmen and pants pressers attracted other showmen who
themselves were ex-bicycle repairers, ex-waiters, ex-stevedores
and ex-messenger boys before they had profited from the nickelodeon and cinema boom. Most of the top jobs on the business
side went to successful exhibitors and salesmen, and increasingly
banking interests demanded and received seats in the New York
boardrooms. And not a few positions in the studios and business
offices went to relatives who entered the industry in prodigious
numbers. At one time it was calculated that there were twenty-
nine members of the Cohn family at Columbia, a dozen Schencks
at Loew's, half-a-dozen relatives of Louis B. Mayer at M-G-M,
and Paramount could almost have staged a football game between
the Zukors and Balabans in its employ; Universal's support of
over a dozen executives drawn from Laemmle's kin inspired the
Ogden Nash lines 'Uncle Carl Laemmle, Has a very large
faemmle'; the Twentieth Century company which became one
of M-G-M's greatest rivals, was founded with money lent by
Nicholas Schenck of Loew's to his brother Joseph, and Louis
Mayer to his son-in-law William Goetz. One could cover several

pages with instances of nepotism, just as one could match them
with stories of family hostility – of Jack Warner's absence from
brother Harry's funeral, or Harry Cohn's pleasure at seeing his
nephew leave Hollywood to run Columbia's television company
in New York ('One bastard at the studio is enough'), of Mayer
cutting William Goetz out of his will, to mention only a few.

Undoubtedly there *was* much nepotism and it was bitterly
resented by outsiders, giving rise to the sour jokes that 'the only
thing a producer produces is relatives', and the old favourite 'the
son-in law also rises'. Some of the nepotism was due to the fact
that the industry's founders still had a small-business mentality
and ran their companies like little family concerns, and there
were plenty of safe jobs around for fast-talking, incompetent
poseurs willing to take the credit for other men's work. On the
other hand some of this nepotism was only apparent: the founding families often intermarried, and their sons and daughters
frequently married inside the closed movie community in which
they were reared.

The industry's chief need as always was for creative talent –
for stars, potential stars, writers, directors, composers, designers,
and all the varied contributors needed to make a movie. Many
were chosen from the thousands of aspirants who came knocking
on the door hoping to break into films. For others the companies
scoured America and reached out over the world. The Swedish
film industry came to a virtual standstill when the directors
Victor Sjöström and Mauritz Stiller were signed up along with
Stiller's protégée Greta Garbo; the two directors were soon dispensed with while Miss Garbo remained as a protegée of Louis
Mayer. Hollywood gravely weakened its major foreign competi-
tor of the silent days, Germany, by tempting the leading German
artists to America. To those whom they courted the moguls
offered irresistibly lucrative contracts and promises of artistic
freedom. The latter usually turned out to be illusory.

The other main need of the industry was for a new kind of
executive to stand between the studio chiefs and the actual film-
makers and to co-ordinate the activities of the specialized departments. This hierarchy was staffed in part by relatives and

by men of the magnates' own kind and more or less their age who had been around for years. Typical of these was Eddie Mannix, a tough Irishman who started out as a bouncer at the New York amusement park owned by Joe and Nick Schenck and finished up as a vice-president of M-G-M. Or Hunt Stromberg, the ex-sports journalist, who was the first person to get a 'produced by' credit at M-G-M. It was Stromberg who is reputed to have said during a studio discussion on a projected Robert Flaherty documentary about the South Seas: 'Boys, I've got an idea. Let's fill the screen with tits.' The rest volunteered or were recruited from all over. Initially there were few with university education or experience in the other arts, which made a man like Walter Wanger, an Ivy League graduate and Broadway producer, something of a rarity. His quiet manner and dignified presence set him apart from his brasher, less literate contemporaries; he became one of the industry's philosophers and spokesmen on many an official occasion and through his 'thoughtful', and partially ghosted) articles in such magazines as *Atlantic Monthly*.

The most striking of the newcomers were the young men born around the turn of the century who came to supervise the making of films at the time when the founding moguls were beginning to flag, to combat their first ulcers and get heart attacks. In 1927 the older men had an intimation of mortality with the death of Marcus Loew at the relatively early age of fifty-seven. An even more striking indication of the toll the movies could take came the following month when, twenty-four hours before the première of *The Jazz Singer*, the man principally responsible for this epoch-making sound movie, Sam Warner, died of a cerebral haemorrhage brought on by the strain of supervising this make-or-break bid by Warners to become a major company. He was only thirty-nine. Many moguls must have felt the way Carl Laemmle did when he collapsed in 1930 during an address to a Universal sales convention: 'I never knew how tired I was until I arrived here yesterday. I found I was completely worn out. I am not sick but just worn out.'

They must have recognized too, without ever being prepared publicly to profess it, their need for men of ideas and ability.

What they were looking for were the kind of people that the banker Joseph Kennedy knew the industry needed. Businessmen could help bring greater efficiency, he argued, but they could not produce movies: 'Movie production requires producers, men with a flair for showmanship and an instinct for dramaturgy, men who can orchestrate the sound and the fury of which pictures are made.' Such people were in short supply. 'Not half a dozen men have ever been able to keep the whole equation of pictures in their heads,' says Cecilia Brady, narrator of *The Last Tycoon*. This is perhaps putting it a little low. But these bustling young men who had grown up with the cinema were always in demand, moving from studio to studio, taking on impossible burdens of work, and sometimes burning themselves out the way Sam Warner did. Their business acumen was considerable, yet they were essentially film-makers, creations of Hollywood and the studio system.

Among the outstanding ones were Hal Wallis, who worked his way up through the Warner Brothers' publicity department; Mark Hellinger, Dore Schary, Jerry Wald and Joseph Mankiewicz who entered as writers after experience in journalism and the theatre; Buddy Adler, reformed playboy son of a New York family who had quit the family business in temporary disgrace; and above all the pre-eminent trio of Irving Thalberg, David O. Selznick and Darryl F. Zanuck, the men for whom Hollywood coined terms like 'boy wonder' and 'boy genius'. A fourth name might be added, that of Walt Disney, who belongs in a unique category as the only person who created a film-making organization based on his own artistic talent. This came about largely through the failure of the reigning moguls to appreciate his worth. Some exaggerated claims have been made for Disney (and there is much to criticize in the later development of his work), but it is difficult to think of any artist who has come anywhere near possessing such business ability. His foresight in pioneering the feature length cartoon, coming to terms with television, and launching the Disneyland amusement park are in marked contrast to the proverbial caution of most moguls.

Although they obviously lacked the genius of a Disney, any

one of the boy wonders could have carved out a reputation as a screenwriter or director. Several of them eventually did. Dore Schary began as a writer, spent twenty years in top production at RKO and M-G-M and returned to the stage as a playwright and director. Joseph Mankiewicz started out in the Paramount script department, and after years as an executive at M-G-M and Twentieth Century-Fox became the writer-producer-director which he had really wanted to be all the time. (He is the man to whom Scott Fitzgerald addressed the classic Hollywood plea: 'Oh Joe, can't producers ever be wrong? I'm a good writer – honest.' Fitzgerald was not, unfortunately, a good *screen*writer, and Mankiewicz was right in the case of the script for *Three Soldiers*.) Thalberg, Zanuck and Selznick might well have done the same, without perhaps reaching the Mankiewicz class. But for them one feels there was (in Zanuck's case still is) a desire for power, to work through other people and control their destinies from the top. The top for Zanuck was the place from which he could push producer Walter Wanger aside on *Cleopatra* and then dictate to the film's director, Joseph Mankiewicz.

There are various ways of getting into the movies: to be born into them, to drift in, to force your way in, to buy your way in, or to be invited in. Thalberg drifted in; Zanuck forced his way in; Selznick was trained in the art of production by his father, Lewis J. Selznick. From their teens they lived in the movie world and had little life outside it. Zanuck was to gain some reputation as a polo player and big game hunter, but of the Riviera set with which he often consorted, he once said: 'They're freaks to me and I'm a freak to them.' All three married inside the profession and had relatives in the business. They had much else in common.

Thalberg and Selznick were both New York Jews, the sons of prosperous immigrants. Thalberg's father was a quiet, comfortably-off lace importer; the family had a legal career in mind for their son but the boy's continual illnesses, culminating in a severe bout of rheumatic fever, forced him to leave school at seventeen to take an undemanding office job. Selznick was reared in the bustle of movie-making, his father an extraordinary buccaneering figure even for a film tycoon. Selznick senior brought up his sons to follow his own philosophy: 'Live expensively! Throw it around! Give it away! Always remember to live beyond your means. It gives a man confidence.' David was destined for Yale; then his father went bust, leaving his boys with a knowledge of the business, tastes they could not afford, and a name guaranteed to close a few Hollywood doors in their faces.

Zanuck comes of mixed English and Swiss stock and was born in Wahoo, Nebraska, where his father was a hotel clerk. His parents split up when he was a child and his mother took him to Los Angeles. Like Thalberg he was small and slight, and looked young for his age. When the twenty-year-old Zanuck was first introduced to Jack Warner he was taken for sixteen; when Norma Shearer first met Thalberg she mistook him for the office boy. Selznick, however, was big and robust; at an inch over six feet he was a tall man by any standards and a positive giant in Hollywood. Oddly enough he invariably attended fancy-dress parties disguised as Theodore Roosevelt, one of America's shortest and most volatile presidents. David was somewhat short-sighted – as were his father and Teddy Roosevelt. Fancy-dress balls, however, were not his favourite recreation. Like the older tycoon generation Selznick and his fellow boy wonders, Thalberg and Zanuck, spent what free time they had at the card tables or watching the roulette wheels spin, always with large sums at stake.

Thalberg's career was the shortest and most meteoric; Selznick's the most publicized and elevated; Zanuck's the most turbulent and sustained.

Irving Thalberg was launched as the result of one of Uncle Carl Laemmle's strange whims. He had been unhappily employed as a clerk in a New York importing firm when a chance encounter with Laemmle at his grandmother's summer cottage brought him into a lowly secretarial job at Universal's New York office. His mother apparently dropped a hint to Mrs Laemmle to secure the job and Laemmle clearly took a liking to the quietly confident young man. He had been less than two years there when, quite on the spur of the moment, Laemmle told him to pack a bag and accompany him to California that day. Thalberg was twenty, an experienced shorthand-typist, and Laemmle had some things to dictate on the way. Two months later, again on the spur of the moment, Laemmle took off for Europe to pursue his philanthropic work on behalf of German post-war relief, leaving Thalberg vaguely in charge of a chaotic Universal City. In a matter of weeks Thalberg had the situation in hand and won his first battle – a showdown with the redoubtable Eric von Stroheim. (He was to encounter Stroheim again at M-G-M and cut down to commercially manageable length the classic movie *Greed* that the Austrian had begun at the Goldwyn studios before the merger. The alleged butchery of this masterpiece and the destruction of the rejected material is among the gravest charges posterity has brought against the boy genius.) Discontented with his 450 dollars a week salary, Thalberg left Universal and joined Louis B. Mayer for an extra 150 dollars in 1923. This was just before Mayer's merger with Metro and Goldwyn. With M-G-M his salary rose to 2,000 dollars a week and then to a guaranteed annual minimum of 400,000 dollars. When he threatened to quit the company as a protest against Nicholas Schenck's willingness to sell Loew's and M-G-M to William Fox, Thalberg is said to have received a straight 250,000 dollars gift from Schenck to soothe his ruffled feelings.

Thalberg was worth it – his pictures earned enough money to justify such rewards. He produced pictures that not merely made money but also brought prestige to the company. He in fact devised the concept of the 'prestige picture', a film that might lose at the box-office yet bring kudos and goodwill to the studio, attracting respectable talent into the company's orbit, generating confidence and giving 'dignity' to the medium. Such a concept incidentally is only possible within a balanced studio output and is similar to the traditional practice of publishing houses, though publishers play for much lower stakes. Thalberg had an almost unerring ability to bring artistic aspiration in line with the demands of the box-office. This finely-judged sense of compromise is perhaps the most important attribute of a successful producer. No one – not even Goldwyn, Zanuck or Selznick – has ever possessed it to quite the same degree as Thalberg. And not only did he possess it, he also had the presence and articulateness to convey it to his fellow producers and artists. He was the reverse of someone like Harry Cohn. Where Cohn was bullying, foul-mouthed and semi-literate, Thalberg was tactful, coolly persuasive, cultivated. Cohn once expressed his undoubted box-office instinct thus: 'When I'm alone in the projection room, I have a foolproof device for judging whether a picture is good or bad. If my fanny squirms, it's bad. If my fanny doesn't squirm, it's good. It's as simple as that.'[1] Thalberg on the other hand was able to say exactly and precisely what he wanted. He never made a film of which he had reason to be ashamed, but the best pictures that came out of Columbia under the Cohn régime have stood the test of time better than those of Thalberg. With a few exceptions the latter strike a modern viewer as ponderous and over-calculated.

The simple fact is that Thalberg was so certain of his own judgment that it hardly ever occurred to him, once he had made up his mind, that he might be wrong. And commercially he seldom was. His interference was rarely arbitrary or niggling. He listened carefully to the opinions of those with whom he worked but there was never any question about whose decision was final. He was quite prepared to double the budget on King Vidor's *The Big Parade* (1925) to make it into a better picture when everyone else in the company had no faith in the box-office potential of a down-beat realistic war movie. At the same time he insisted upon being present for the rehearsals of major scenes in his productions before they were shot, and his practice of re-editing films after previews led to the famous remark: 'Irving doesn't make films, he remakes them.' One can see the effect of his heavy pro-

---

[1]This story is told so often *against* Cohn that it is worth pointing out that Fritz Lang cites the story as an instance of the Columbia president's acumen. He was present at a preview which concluded with Cohn telling a director: 'This is a very good picture, but it is exactly nineteen minutes too long... Young man, exactly nineteen minutes ago my ass started to itch and right there I know the audience would feel the same.' Says Lang: 'And he was quite right! The moment an audience starts to itch around you have lost them'. (*Fritz Lang in America* by Peter Bogdanovich, London, Studio Vista, 1969, p. 88).

duction hand at its most pronounced by comparing the films made by the Marx brothers at Paramount with those they starred in at M-G-M, which they joined in 1934. Thalberg sent them on the road to try out their big scenes on live audiences, had vulgar big-scale musical numbers injected into the contrived scenarios, and although the result had far greater professional polish and featured many a memorable scene, the Marx brothers were robbed of much of their original vitality and spontaneity.

Naturally he made some mistakes, the most famous of them being his miscalculation over Tod Browning's *Freaks* (1932). Thalberg respected Browning and, against considerable opposition in the studio, backed his circus thriller with its cast of genuine dwarfs and physically deformed characters, in the belief that the public, as he did, would recognize the honesty, sympathy and sincerity of Browning's treatment. Sadly he wholly misjudged the public response: audiences ran screaming from the cinema, the film was mutilated by local censors and denied an exhibition certificate in Great Britain until 1963. So outraged were most M-G-M top executives that the company's name was removed from the beginning of the film. The professional setback for Browning was considerable: some would even say fatal. In backing *Freaks,* however, Thalberg had overestimated the intelligence of the film-going public, and not set out to exploit its taste for the bizarre. The film is widely regarded today as something of a classic.

Thalberg's utter dedication to making good films and money won him respect on both sides of the industry. Largely as a result of his presence and influence, M-G-M became the most successful, most prestigious studio in Hollywood, noted for its glossy style, professional finish and vast roster of stars ('More Stars than there are in Heaven', was the company's slogan). Without him Louis B. Mayer would not have achieved the distinction he did. Mayer came to regard Thalberg as a son, despite the inevitable jealousy that arose. This paternal feeling was later transferred to his son-in-law David Selznick and, more briefly, to his last assistant (and successor) Dore Schary.

Like most movie executives Thalberg was a difficult man to

get to see : the seats in his reception office became known as the Million Dollar Bench because of the hours and even days that highly-paid employees spent there waiting for an audience. King Vidor tells an extraordinary story about Thalberg conducting a script conference on a projected Western movie on the way to, during, and returning from a film star's funeral.

This total absorption took its toll. Thalberg was never a fit man and the unrelenting pressure of work, along with the refusal of Mayer and Schenck to give him any relief, resulted in a series of breakdowns. He was also getting depressed with the studio system itself, and particularly the lowering of standards at M-G-M and elsewhere in the face of the depression. He despised the shoddy catch-penny work that was being turned out, and the desperate resort to triple bills of mediocre pictures being shown to lure people back into the cinemas. He told the producer of one such exploitation movie which he particularly disliked, despite its success with a pre-view audience: 'You've got a smash hit. A few more like that and you'll smash the industry.' Yet he never let up. Those who worked with him report on the complete command he showed of a hundred aspects of dozens of movies being shot and planned, when they came to discuss them. 'You would be working with your writer,' the director Clarence Brown has testified, 'and you would come to this scene in the script. It didn't click. It just didn't jell. The scene was no goddam good. You would make a date with Irving, talk to him for thirty minutes, and you'd come away from his office with the best scene in the picture.' Waxy faced, almost corpse-like in appearance, sometimes too tired to get up from his desk, he could switch his mind from one task to another and indicated a grasp of the smallest detail presented to him, even if his punctiliousness struck some cynical observers as absurd in its often humourless pondering on seeming triviality. Not that Thalberg was without a sense of humour : he was noted in his early days for the crispness of his repartee and for his occasional whimsicalities, in marked contrast to the folksiness and lewd banter of Louis Mayer. (In one of his celebrated encounters with Stroheim, Thalberg viewed a lengthy sequence from *The Merry Widow* featuring a seemingly endless series of shots of boots, shoes, slippers and other footwear piled in a cupboard. 'I want to establish that this man is a foot fetishist,' explained the director. 'You are a footage fetishist,' cracked Thalberg.) But latterly he found little to laugh at around the M-G-M lot.

Thalberg planned to move into independent production as soon as his unbreakable contract was completed. But in 1936, at the age of thirty-seven, his health gravely undermined by overwork, he died of pneumonia. In splendidly ambivalent Hollywood fashion he passed on whispering the Lord's Prayer, had his funeral at Rabbi Magnin's Jewish Temple, and was buried in Forest Lawn cemetery. At that point the man who had become a legend in the film industry in his brief lifetime was ready for virtual canonization. Charles MacArthur, the playwright, described M-G-M without Thalberg: it was 'like going to the automat'. The following year the imposing white marble executive block on the Culver City lot was named The Irving Thalberg Memorial Building, and a new Academy Award, 'The Irving Thalberg Memorial Award', was instituted for especially ditinguished production, and not necessarily to be presented each year. The first recipient was Darryl Zanuck, who has had it twice since, followed by Hal Wallis, David Selznick and Walt Disney. Fitzgerald's *The Last Tycoon* was to put the final seal of approval on the wonder boy. Nevertheless a question remains, and it is put succinctly by Bosley Crowther in his history of Metro-Goldwyn-Mayer:

> There is no way of telling how much the lasting cult of Thalberg is a compound of genuine admiration for what he was and what he did, or a wistful, almost pitiful, manifestation of the community's hunger for comforting symbols of its own worth.

Thalberg had left one film to be released after his death. And when *The Good Earth* was shown it carried a foreword: 'To the memory of Irving Grant Thalberg we dedicate this picture – his last great achievement.' Seldom before had his name appeared on a movie; he had felt no need to demonstrate his power in that way. His assurance and lack of ostentation were undoubtedly among the attributes that made him a legend in a community where self-advertisement was a way of life.

No one has ever accused Darryl Zanuck or David Selznick of hiding their lights under a bushel of other people's credits. Whoever wrote or directed one of their pictures, the names of Zanuck and Selznick were as big or bigger than anyone else's, and usually up there above the title. Whereas Thalberg had begun his Hollywood career virtually at the top, Zanuck and Selznick started off as humble labourers in the vineyards of, respectively, the Warner Brothers and Louis B. Mayer. Zanuck's first contact with the cinema was in 1914 when at the age of eleven he earned a dollar-a-day playing an Indian maiden in a Western. After the war he tried to break into the industry as a writer. He sold a few scripts but the sudden influx of well-known novelists and playwrights pushed him briefly into the Los Angeles shipyards as a riveter's mate. Then Zanuck decided that if it was necessary to be a published author to win the respect of the studios, he would become one. So he took three of his rejected screenplays, turned them into stories and persuaded a hair tonic firm to back their publication as a book called *Habit*. In return for this support he dropped in several plugs for the company's product ('Yuccatone') and added a testimonial to its efficacy. Incredibly there were immediate bids for the screen rights of the stories, and Zanuck's career had begun. Soon he was the most active writer at Warner Brothers, specializing in scripts for the studio's most important performer, the canine star Rin Tin Tin. He wrote so much that he had to resort to pseudonyms. Some indication of Zanuck's value can be seen in Jack Warner's autobiographical reflection on the firm's fortunes in 1922: 'We had one continuing problem at our Sunset lot – a persistent lack of money, popular stars and story ideas.' From being a mere writer, he graduated to production assignments in a studio that almost overnight became a major company through its successful gamble in introducing sound. The big jump came when he was promoted to head of production at Warners in 1929, a job he held until 1933 at a salary of 5,000 dollars a week. Over these years he grew an imposing military moustache (to which in the second world war he added the commissioned rank of lieutenant-colonel) and shed a stammer that had dogged him since childhood. At Warners he was succeeded by Hal Wallis who himself later left to run his own independent unit.

The official reason for Zanuck's departure was the refusal of Harry Warner to restore the fifty per cent emergency salary cut that had been made for all studio personnel to meet the fall of business in the early depression. But beyond this was a growing friction between himself and Jack Warner, both spikey, aggressive personalities, unwilling to share the credit with each other and yet supposedly working on level terms. (Nevertheless in 1961 when Richard Zanuck's production of *The Chapman Report* was cancelled a week before shooting commenced at Twentieth Century-Fox, it took only one call from his father in Paris to Jack Warner in Hollywood to have the multi-million dollar film shifted immediately to the Warner studio.)

For an ordinary American 1933 was a bad year to find oneself out of work. Zanuck was, and continues to be, no ordinary American. Almost immediately he embarked upon the major phase of his career, the creation in association with Joseph Schenck of the Twentieth Century Company. On the face of it, this was a ridiculous time to found a new company; perhaps no one but Schenck could have raised the money for such an undertaking, and few besides Zanuck could have made it a success. With Wallace Beery, borrowed from M-G-M, for the first major film *The Bowery* they were off to a good start, and with the rapid addition of the shaky Fox company with its chain of theatres, Twentieth Century-Fox was one of America's top four movie companies. From 1933 until 1956 Zanuck was (except for a couple of years in the war) vice-president in charge of production. He also became and remained the company's largest individual stockholder. Over these years he maintained a consistently profitable level of production, mixing good films with trash. His best films had a pungent topical appeal. At Warners he had helped initiate the gangster and 'social conscience' cycles with pictures like *Little Caesar* (1930) and *I am a Fugitive From a Chain Gang* (1932) that shaped

Warners' studio style for nearly two decades. He now moved towards a more serious treatment of contemporary life in *The Grapes of Wrath* (1940) and, after the war, the semi-documentary thrillers and films on race prejudice. Not to be outdone, however, by the hordes of child stars swarming around the knees of Louis B. Mayer, Twentieth Century-Fox was also the home of Shirley Temple, and the source of glossy romance, trite historical pieces (utterly inferior to Warners), and corny comedies.

In pursuing his aims Zanuck was autocratic to a degree ('For God's sake don't say yes until I've finished talking') and a powerhouse of energy, working an eighteen-hour day. As with other moguls he was not a receptive man when it came to criticism. Fox was not the only company in the history of Hollywood to withdraw its advertising as a protest against adverse reviews; every company did this at one time or another when all other means had been exhausted. Fox is, however, probably the only company that went to the length of hiring a film critic as a Hollywood script adviser to prevent him from criticizing their films any further. This was how the late Frank Nugent, movie critic of *The New York Times*, became a screenwriter.

By the mid-fifties, with television bringing a production slowdown, the excitement of running a major studio was beginning to wear off for Zanuck. He had been one of the first tycoons to start using frozen currency to produce movies in Europe, and he resigned as a production chief to set himself up as an independent producer to make films for Twentieth Century-Fox release from a base in Paris. He was succeeded by Buddy Adler who had recently joined the company from Columbia. Financially the following five years were lean ones for Zanuck. Picture after picture received poor reviews and showed indifferent returns at the box-office; his ideas and interventions had been useful over a range of studio productions, but he proved a baleful influence on the individual films he now superintended.

Meanwhile Twentieth Century-Fox itself, after a couple of good years with its widescreen CinemaScope process, was beginning to settle in a mire of maladministration and indecisive leadership. A succession of disastrous flops culminated in the fiasco of *Cleopatra,* which had begun as a relatively minor venture and escalated into the most absurdly expensive film of all time. Buddy Adler had died in 1960, and president Spyros Skouras was worn out. When Zanuck put in his bid for the presidency his reputation was at low ebb and his current independent production *The Longest Day* well behind schedule and way over budget. But 1962 proved for Zanuck to be as important a year as 1933. After a complicated power struggle he replaced the ageing, exhausted Skouras as head of the Twentieth Century-Fox board and saw *The Longest Day* launched on its way to becoming the most profitable black-and-white film ever made. His return gave him a new lease of life, enabling him to get over the prolonged and embarrassing affair with the French singer Juliette Greco, whom he had unsuccessfully attempted to make into a world star, and to rid himself of a drinking problem. But he never went back to Hollywood: instead he placed his son Richard in charge of production – an appointment that has proved a notable success. Why he returned to Twentieth Century-Fox cannot wholly be explained in terms of protecting his own investment in the company. Power played a part certainly, even at an age when anyone else might be considering retirement rather than re-entering the fray. Yet one must also give some credence to his own explanation: 'Pride, that's it, more than anything else pride.' And ultimately his pride was in the continuing achievement of the organization he had created rather than in any individual films he might make outside it.

Very different from this was the attitude of David Selznick, who from the beginning of his career believed in independent production. His first few years of film-making were as undistinguished as Zanuck's. After his father went bankrupt in 1923, David made a couple of short exploitation pictures in New York; the first was about the world heavyweight contender Luis Angel Firpo, called 'Will He Conquer Dempsey?' (a question soon answered in the negative), and the second a two-reeler of Rudolph Valentino judging a beauty contest at Madison Square Gardens. These brought in a quick 16,000 dollars which he immediately lost in an ill-fated attempt to start a publishing house and a flutter in Florida real estate. Penniless, he set out for the West Coast. His father's one-time partner and now sworn enemy Louis B. Mayer refused him employment, but Nicholas Schenck prevailed on Mayer to give him a job. Schenck apparently felt himself under an obligation to David. The story is that as a small boy David had accompanied his father to Schenck's office to discuss a film deal and with childish candour had interjected: 'I shouldn't have anything to do with it, Mr Schenck', a piece of advice that the future president of Loew's Inc. had had no cause to regret taking. For his first couple of years at M-G-M Selznick was an assistant producer of B-feature Westerns. In view of his subsequent extravagance it is interesting to note that his major contribution was to devise a method of cutting production costs by making two pictures at the same time, thus bringing in two movies at 90,000 dollars instead of one at 80,000. This commended him more to the financiers than to Irving Thalberg who cared little for this undignified aspect of the company's activities. And Mayer still distrusted anyone with the name of Selznick, telling his daughter Irene with characteristic elegance and foresight: 'Keep away from that schnook. He'll be a bum, just like his old man.'

In 1929 Selznick provoked a row with Thalberg in the M-G-M executive dining room, the ostensible cause of it being Thalberg's refusal to make him supervisor (the title at that time for the post of producer) of a major film. The upshot was his resignation and move to Paramount to work under B. P. Schulberg. Ben Schulberg, father of novelist Budd, had started out as a publicity man for Adolph Zukor back in 1912, and had been an independent producer during the early 'twenties. While in independent production he discovered 'the IT girl', Clara Bow. He quickly suspected Selznick of being after his job and once told him to his face: 'You're the most arrogant young man I've ever known.' The recognition of the boy wonders' ability was invariably accompanied by jealousy and fear on the part of the older generation. Yet it was a group of financiers from above and not pressure from below that dismissed Schulberg and sent him on the road to oblivion. Looking back on his days with Schulberg thirty years later, Selznick said:

When I was at Paramount years ago we made fifty-two pictures a year and our executive judgments and prejudices and attitudes were stamped on every one of them. You can't make top pictures that way. You can only make assembly-line pictures. You can't make good pictures by a committee system, filtering them through the minds of half-a-dozen men. Besides, salaried people are not so likely to come up with big hits.

At this juncture Selznick was unable to get the necessary backing to go independent. Not without reason he believed that Mayer (now his father-in-law) was responsible, and also suspected Mayer of putting Joe Schenck up to offering him an executive job at United Artists. Determined to make it alone, he refused Schenck's offer and instead joined the struggling RKO where within two years he was head of production and instrumental in pulling the company out of its slump. Reluctantly Mayer changed his opinion, and while Thalberg was convalescing abroad brought David back to M-G-M, this time as vice-president. The appointment caused considerable resentment among the Thalberg faction; some observers date the origin of the 'son-in-law also rises' jibe from this time. Certainly Selznick felt uneasy and after two hugely successful years he broke away to start his own company, Selznick International. Mayer was dead against this move, but Selznick told him bluntly: 'I'm thirty-two and I can afford to fail.'

By now his record was sufficiently well-known for him to have little difficulty raising the necessary money; among the investors in the company were Irving Thalberg and his wife, the M-G-M star Norma Shearer. Soon Selznick was an independent producer to rank alongside Samuel Goldwyn. His greatest triumph came early and the rest of his career was something of an anti-climax. Towards the end of his life he even suggested his own epitaph: 'Here lies David O. Selznick who produced *Gone With the Wind.*'

No one had spent as much money on a picture before as Selznick spent on *Gone With the Wind,* and no independent producer at the time would have dared embark on such a venture. Its making revealed the obsessional quality Selznick brought to his pictures. In the course of filming he used three main directors and fifteen writers, as well as doing a great deal of writing and some direction himself. He would often go for days without sleep and kept up a ceaseless barrage of letters and memoranda to his hirelings. One calls them hirelings not because Selznick failed to respect them but because writers and directors were people he engaged to do a job exactly the way he wanted it done. A typical reaction of Selznick was that of his friend Nunnally Johnson in turning down a scripting job: 'My understanding is that an assignment from you consists of three months' work and six months' recuperation'. And Selznick himself summed up his approach to the cinema when he fired director George Cukor off *Gone With the Wind*: 'Your ideas may be right, but if I'm going to fall flat on my face, it's going to be my own mistake.' Like Thalberg he was contemptuous of those who saw films merely as a money-making venture, but he had this brutal retort for those who scorned commerce entirely: 'If you are primarily concerned with something that is usually called personal artistic integrity, you don't belong in the business of making commercial pictures. You should get yourself a paint-brush or a typewriter.'

Although his standing within the industry always remained high, Selznick's reputation rests on his first ten years as an independent producer, and primarily on the success of *Gone With the Wind* which ranks with *Birth of a Nation* as one of the most profitable films ever made.[2] After *Duel in the Sun* (1947) he lost his touch, the firm ran into debt and after his first batch of post-war films Selznick never worked in Hollywood again. He wound up the company and in five years paid off his creditors by re-releasing his old pictures and hiring them to television. He travelled a great deal and was always full

---

[2]Currently this title is held by *The Sound of Music* which has grossed over 70,000,000 dollars in North America alone as against *Gone With the Wind's* 47,000,000. However one must bear in mind both devaluation and the vast increase in seat prices, and also the possibility that the current re-release of *Gone With the Wind*, now blown up to 70 mm., might restore its pre-eminent position. In the case of *Birth of a Nation* no satisfactory records were kept of its astronomical returns, though it is in fact almost certainly the biggest draw of all time.

of grandiose schemes such as a film of *War and Peace,* which he was beaten to by an Italian company, and a life of Mary Magdalene. It was while working on the latter that a screenwriter discovered Selznick had never actually read the New Testament and accordingly set about reading the Gospels aloud to him. As the writer was running through the beatitudes, Selznick's eye was taken by a bulldozer clearing a building site down in the valley below them. 'I wouldn't have minded a piece of that real estate,' said Selznick; the writer threw the good book at him.

In Europe Selznick was concerned with three pictures of which two, starring his new wife Jennifer Jones, proved disastrous (*Gone to Earth* and *Terminal Station*), and one (*The Third Man*) a critical and box-office success. Although, as he said, he did 'little that contributed to its success', Selznick was not above re-editing *The Third Man* for American distribution. After nine years he actually produced a film single-handed, a re-make of Hemingway's *A Farewell to Arms,* financed by Twentieth Century-Fox, and made in Italy. The old Selznick frenzy returned undiminished. He fired off a record ten thousand memos ranging in length from a sentence to thirty pages (a selection of them was published in *Life* magazine with his approval), exhausted three secretaries, sacked director John Huston, and fell out with his screenwriter and life-long friend Ben Hecht. To little avail. For the picture proved a staggering flop and provided yet another nail for Spyros Skouras' coffin.

After the failure of *A Farewell to Arms* Selznick continued with his plans. When he died seven years later none of them had got on to a studio floor. At the time of his death his agent was running advertisements in the trade press to keep his reputation alive. And on the day the acute coronary struck and sent him to join Irving Thalberg in Forest Lawn, an advertisement in *Hollywood Reporter* ended plaintively: 'Come back DOS, the industry needs you'.

During the 'fifties Selznick's old studio M-G-M put out a picture called *The Bad and the Beautiful* concerning the attempted come-back of a ruthless tycoon, Jonathan Shields, who – correctly or not – was widely taken to be modelled on Selznick. One doubts that the picture would have been made at M-G-M under Mayer who a couple of years earlier had stormed out of a preview of Billy Wilder's *Sunset Boulevard*, shouting: 'We should horsewhip this Wilder, we should throw him out of this town that is feeding him'. Yet as films about Hollywood tend to be, *The Bad and the Beautiful* was pretty ambivalent. Novels have on the whole handled the movie colony more harshly; their authors, belonging to what for many years was the most ill-treated, exploited and disregarded profession in the industry, often had debts to settle. At most studios writers were treated like serfs, forced to keep office hours and very rarely left to work alone on a script. The practice, developed in the first place by Irving Thalberg, of several writers working unknown to each other on the same screenplay, was widespread. Even today it is rare for a screenplay to be the work of a single author, although a good many of the worst abuses were checked by the rise of the Screenwriters Guild, the formation of which was impeded at every stage by the moguls.

The two best-known Hollywood novels deal in extremes of boy wonders. On the one hand is Fitzgerald's *The Last Tycoon*, featuring the noble Monroe Stahr, the producer as hero, who stands for all that is best in the Hollywood system. On the other hand is Budd Schulberg's *What Makes Sammy Run?* featuring Sammy Glick, the producer as heel, who stands for all that is worst. Both books were being written at the same time by men who knew each other well, and indeed the background of Cecilia Brady in *The Last Tycoon* is partly composed of what Schulberg told Fitzgerald of his own Hollywood childhood. In choosing a father for his own narrator, Schulberg went to the other end of the spectrum from the tough movie pioneer Ben Schulberg and made Al Mannheim's father a quiet New England small-town rabbi.

Both writers were Marxists (Schulberg actually a Communist Party member when he wrote the book) but there were certain differences as well as complementary factors in their reading of the situation. Fitzgerald, a romantic to the last, saw his hero as the dying representative of a vital tradition. Schulberg, equally romantic in his way, viewed the likes of Sammy Glick, a creation of capitalist society, as standing in the way of the glories that a great people's art could offer in the future. When we move to the real situation behind this fictional polarity, conclusions are less easily drawn.

The character of Monroe Stahr is based quite closely on Irving Thalberg, and the force of *The Last Tycoon* as a historical document (as opposed to a self-contained work of art, which despite its incompleteness it is, and of a major order) depends upon the Thalberg legend. *What Makes Sammy Run?* is always said to have been inspired by the early career of Jerry Wald, though Schulberg has claimed that Sammy could have been a dozen other people as well, and no doubt partly was. Certainly the notoriously glib, credit-stealing opportunist that Wald was in his youth suggests Sammy Glick, but Wald was neither as totally unscrupulous nor as untalented. Yet up to his death in 1962, at the age of fifty, he was never able to shake off the identification any more than one is able to put Monroe Stahr entirely out of mind in examining the life of Thalberg. 'For years I've been fighting the Sammy Glick image,' Wald once told Schulberg. 'People thought I was Sammy. Let me tell you something: Sammy Glick was a boy scout leader compared to Harry Cohn.' There can be little doubt that Wald was, to put it mildly, a man of lesser stature than Thalberg. Nonetheless, his production record is not to be despised. He worked as an executive producer (and later in charge of his own unit) at Warner Brothers, RKO, Columbia and Twentieth Century-Fox, respected by the actual filmmakers whom he protected from the studio bosses. And if he had a reputation for making off with other people's ideas, he was not noted for wanton interference in their work. Anyway, he received the Irving Thalberg Memorial Award in 1948.

Wald died in the middle of the confusion that reigned at Twentieth Century-Fox during the making of *Cleopatra*, and in a letter written a couple of days before his death to the Fox publicity man on that film he said:

19 The independent Paramount-based producer Hal Wallis (left) with Dore Schary, vice-president in charge of production at M-G-M, in ebullient mood on the occasion of the unveiling of Paramount's widescreen process VistaVision, that was introduced after the enormous success of 20th Century-Fox's CinemaScope in 1953. Despite Schary's smile, VistaVision was not greatly in demand at M-G-M's Culver City.

20 Irving Thalberg, the original Boy Wonder and model for Scott Fitzgerald's Monroe Stahr, poses in the obligatory southern California pool with his wife, the M-G-M star Norma Shearer.

21 John Wayne, producer Walter Wanger and his wife, actress Joan Bennett, at a 1941 United Artists sales convention held at Mary Pickford's lavish Hollywood mansion 'Pickfair'. Two years earlier, Wanger's *Stagecoach* had launched Wayne into gun-toting stardom; ten years later Wanger pulled a gun on his wife's agent and went to gaol.

22 A pensive David Selznick dining out with Joan Bennett in the 1930s at which time Miss Bennett was affecting the fashionable blonde hair-do.

23 David O. Selznick, son of pioneer tycoon Lewis Selznick in the early twenties when his father was still in business and David was on the threshold of his meteoric career.

24 The youthful Darryl F. Zanuck, vice-president in charge of production at 20th Century-Fox, introduces his company's new acquisition, the Norwegian skating star Sonja Henie, to the London press in the late thirties.

25 The mature Zanuck and his protégée, the French chanteuse Juliette Greco, take a break from the gambling tables at the Casino Bellevue, Biarritz, in 1958. At this time Zanuck was operating as an independent producer in Paris; he returned to New York in 1962 to oust Spyros Skouras from the presidency of 20th Century-Fox.

Right now, the studio is filled with chaos, confusion, contradictions and just plain old fashioned crap. I wish they'd settle the presidency so we can all go back to work. As far as I'm concerned I wish Zanuck would get the job because he's the only one who has the energy, the initiative, the respect – and, most of all – stock, to push everything through that should be pushed through. The great tragedy here at Fox is not so much the pictures we made but the pictures we didn't make.

And he ended the letter with a message to be passed on to *Cleopatra*'s harassed originator and producer Walter Wanger: 'Please tell Walter to take it easy. Ulcers are not becoming to producers.'

6

THE CZAR

I have sometimes thought that a part of the
value I may have had for the industry was the
fact, despite my long residence in New York,
that I have somehow remained an unreconstructed
Middle Westerner from 'the sticks'.

Will H. Hays

8 December 1921 is a crucial date in the history of Hollywood.
On this day a group of fugitives from the pale of czarist Russia
sought out a man as different from themselves as they could have
imagined and invited him to be their czar. Or more prosaically,
the members of the newly constituted Motion Picture Producers
and Distributors of America Inc. invited Will H. Hays to be their
president. The form of the invitation was a round robin signed
by all the major moguls and presented to Hays by a carefully
selected duo: the flamboyant producer Lewis J. Selznick and the
conservative attorney Saul Rogers.

In accepting the offer Hays was doubtless influenced by the
prospect of earning 100,000 dollars a year. He was also moved
by a sense of mission; in his initial statement to the press he spoke
of guiding the industry to 'its predestined place of importance in
the civilization of today and tomorrow'. Hays was installed as
president in March 1922 for a period of five years, and with an
increase of salary to an annual 150,000 dollars he remained the
industry's official spokesman, prime trouble-shooter and final
arbiter until his retirement in 1945. During his period as president
the MPPDA (changed in 1945 to MPAA for Motion Pic-
ture Association of America Inc.) was known as the Hays Office
and the Production Code governing movie morality as the Hays
Office Code.

In founding the MPPDA the tycoons were making a last desperate bid to set aside their personal differences – or rather
temporarily to conceal them – and put their house in order before

a growing pressure for public regulation became irresistible. In choosing Hays they clearly had in mind the image they wished to present. For while many of the criticisms directed at the disorganized industry and the restrictive measures proposed were amply justified, there was lurking beneath some of them a strong current of xenophobia that frequently broke through to the surface. A typical instance of the sort of attack the tycoons encountered every day is this report from a 1920 newspaper: 'The lobby of the International Reform Bureau, Dr Wilbur Crafts presiding, voted tonight to rescue the motion pictures from the hands of the Devil and five hundred un-Christian Jews.'

In discussions preceding the invitation to Hays, frequent reference was made to the success of the recently enthroned 'czar of baseball', Judge Kenesaw Mountain Landis, who had been appointed special baseball commissioner after gambling interests had fixed the 1919 World Series. Landis, a solid midwestern jurist of formidable mien, was a celebrated reactionary and his very name sufficient to restore public faith in the probity of baseball. The movie industry was looking for just such a man to carry out an infinitely more complicated task and in Hays they found their ideal czar.

Hays was just about everything that Fox, Laemmle, Goldwyn, Zukor, Selznick, and the other signatories of the round robin were not. He was a thin, jug-eared, abstemious midwesterner, a proud descendant from one of the earliest families to settle in Indiana, able (and ever ready) to boast of his pure Anglo-Saxon stock. A graduate of Wabash College (the institution that fired Ezra Pound for breaches of its stern morality), a partner in the family's small-town law firm, a presbyterian elder (H. L. Mencken always referred to him contemptuously as 'Elder Hays'), he had been national chairman of the Republican Party at the 1920 convention that nominated the prophet of 'normalcy' Warren Harding. His reward had been a place in President Harding's cabinet as Postmaster-General. Ironically enough this cabinet was itself to be exposed as the source of scandal in the famous Teapot Dome oil affair. Equally ironically, in the early 'twenties the Indiana state government fell into the hands of the most virulent northern branch of the Ku Klux Klan, the post-war revival of which as a focus for small-town xenophobia can in some measure be attributed to the popularity of D. W. Griffith's *Birth of a Nation*. In Indiana the Klan's activities were directed almost entirely against Jews and Catholics, which is to say against the people who hired Hays and against those to whom he was shortly to turn for guidance.

So whatever the problems posed by his new job, Hays was well out of both his home state and the national capital. And as executive head of the MPPDA he was given a free hand to appoint his own staff and run his operation as he saw fit. For diplomatic reasons his staff was composed entirely of Anglo-Saxon protestants, usually those who had held some previous public office, and influential Catholic laymen. Naturally he set up his headquarters in New York where the ultimate power lay. From this vantage point he analysed the situation and broke it down into ten specific problems he had to solve: internal disorders (e.g. bad trade practices and scandals); censorship and other threatened restrictions; foreign crises, the most pressing being the Mexican government's refusal to admit American movies; the building of what he called 'a more perfect union' within the industry that would be the basis of self-regulation; a rapid improvement in the quality of movies; the creation of a public demand for better movies; an improvement in the quality of advertising; turning the current hostility of educationalists into practical co-operation; helping distributors to overcome fraud and loss; assisting exhibitors to adjust contract problems.

His first domestic successes came in the fight against censorship for which much of the credit must go to the MPPDA's first secretary, Courtland Smith, a former president of the American Press Association. Smith worked tirelessly, lecturing, lobbying and cajoling across the country, and was personally responsible for an overwhelming defeat of a film censorship bill before the Massachussetts state legislature. Hays's other immediate triumph was his first exercise in international relations, an agreement with Mexico not to offend that sensitive country and to keep a permanent representative in Mexico City to deal with future prob-

lems. On a less spectacular level Hays set about cleaning up mal-
practices that had for long seemed insoluble. To look into the
theft of films (i.e. exhibition without payment) and similar frauds,
he hired the Burns Detective Agency.

Above all he was determined to be no mere piece of window
dressing, not, as he put it, to be the 'lobbyist, mouthpiece or
fixer' that sceptical observers had predicted. Nor was he there
only to bring order out of chaos, although a person without his
immense gifts for diplomacy and administration would have retired defeated after a month in office. He resolved to put his
mark on the character of the movies themselves as he made
abundantly clear during his first visit to Hollywood in the summer
of 1922.

On his arrival in Los Angeles he was greeted at the station by
Jesse L. Lasky and Joseph Schenck, and for a week was accorded
the kind of reception customarily reserved for royalty. When he
visited studios all work stopped as he addressed assembled
employees; world-famous stars went out of their way to impress
him (Eric von Stroheim struck him as 'one of Hollywood's most
genial souls, though not without a strain of Rabelais'); and his
visit was climaxed by a vast gathering of film people in the recently
opened Hollywood Bowl. At a press conference in Hollywood
Hays made one of his most frequently quoted and characteristic
statements:

This industry must have towards that sacred thing, the mind of the
child, towards that clean virgin thing, that unmarked slate, the same
responsibility, the same care about the impressions made upon it, that
the best clergyman or the most inspired teacher of youth would have.

Such sentiments must have provoked a cynical chuckle at Hollywood parties after his departure and twelve years passed before
Hays managed to translate them into commandments. During
his first few years in office his principal effect on Hollywood was
less on the movies themselves than on the off-screen conduct
of the stars. A series of minor scandals had culminated in three
major ones with which Hays had to contend in his initial twelve
months in office. The first was the murder, still unsolved, of the

English director William Desmond Taylor, an unsavoury affair involving drugs, sexual perversion, and two movie heroines, Mary Miles Minter and Mabel Normand. The second was the arraignment of popular comedian Roscoe 'Fatty' Arbuckle on a manslaughter charge (originally investigated as rape and murder). The third was the death in an asylum of the matinee idol Wallace Reid in the course of an attempt to cure his drug addiction. Although no charges were preferred against Minter or Normand, and Arbuckle was acquitted, their reputations were seriously tarnished; consequently they were sacrificed on the altar of Hollywood's new respectability. Joseph Schenck, who produced Arbuckle's movies, and Adolph Zukor, who distributed them, agreed with Hays to take an enormous loss by suppressing the portly comic's unshown films. In view of the pressure their action is understandable; when a few months later Hays generously lifted the official ban on Arbuckle (to enable him to write and direct, but not to act) there was a national outcry which severely shook him. The support he received in the liberal press was insufficient to compensate for the denunciations from pulpits throughout the land. Henceforth a morality clause was written into every Hollywood contract. The effect was to make the movie colony somewhat more discreet in its behaviour, at least for a while. However, as time passed and national mores changed, a point was reached when the only aspect of a studio employee's private life that had any public importance was his political allegiances.

At the end of Hays's first year the moguls had every reason to be pleased with their choice. Particularly gratifying to them must have been a New York dinner arranged by assorted public dignitaries to honour the two czars – Judge Landis and Will Hays – in whose hands the national sport and the national entertainment medium were now so safe. Certainly Hays was on their side of the industry, as one might have expected of a man who helped elect a president who promised 'a return to normalcy' and was the friend of another who believed that 'the business of America is business'.

On an administrative level Hays's contribution to Hollywood

cannot be over-rated. He was responsible, for example, for such important innovations as the Central Casting Bureau, title registration, and the Labor Committee. If the industry remained over-all in a confused state the blame hardly lies with Hays – he at least helped raise it above the penny-arcade style organization of 1921. But he was not popular among the people who actually made the movies. Like most men of his age and background he had a deep distrust of artists, foreigners and intellectuals, and a hostility towards social change. His personal standards were 'the Ten Commandments, self-discipline, faith in times of trouble, worship, the Bible and the Golden Rule – all of which we might well practise more fully today'. These traditional values which he so notably embodied seemed to be imperiled on all sides, though 'hosts of Americans clung firmly to their own ideals and strongly resisted the alien invasion'. To him a good many of the artists in Hollywood were parties to this 'alien invasion', trouble-makers to be curbed – 'the pseudo-sophisticates in our midst', who were forever trying to put something across on the great American public. In fact there was an unbridgeable gulf between himself and the more independent-minded element in Holly-wood, once described by him revealingly as 'the rank and file of directors and minor studio officials'. The result was a running battle that lasted throughout Hays's period of office. He was not always in the wrong; from his own standpoint he never was.

Certainly one of his most important tasks when he came to the movies was to introduce some form of self-censorship. This pledge was made forcefully in the initial campaign to defeat public control of the industry, and it was enshrined in the MPPDA's articles of incorporation which stated that the primary purpose of the organization was 'to foster the common interest of those engaged in the motion picture industry in the United States by establishing and maintaining the highest possible moral and artistic standards in motion picture production'. To implement this the 'Hays Formula' was devised, by which studios submitted books, scripts and stories to the Hays Office before purchase. This system did not work particularly well, and the appointment of Carl E. Milliken, an ex-governor of Maine and a staid New

Englander, did little to soften the increasing pressure of religious, professional and ethnic groups. It was followed by the adoption of an informal code of 'Don'ts and Be Carefuls', and the introduction into the Hays Office of the diminutive sexagenarian Alice Ames Winter. Mrs Winter, virtually self-appointed, claimed to be spokesman for 'the women of the world' and kept a sharp look-out for anything in the movies that might give offence to her far-flung constituency. She remained at her desk until she had turned eighty, a bitter joke among Hollywood intellectuals and known locally as the 'czarina'.

It was the coming of sound, with its added possibilities of verbal offence, and the tremendous influx of new writers unaccustomed to and unwilling to accept the prohibitions many Hollywood hacks took for granted, that brought into being the so-called 'Hays Office Code'. The Code itself was not of the czar's own devising. Originally it was drafted in 1929 by two midwestern Roman Catholics, Martin Quigley, the Chicago publisher of leading film trade magazines (e.g. *Motion Picture Daily*, *Motion Picture Herald*), and the Rev. Daniel A. Lord sj, a teacher of English and drama at St Louis University and one of the 'technical advisers' (with the protestant clergyman Dr George Reid Andrews and that Hollywood favourite, Rabbi F. Magnin) on DeMille's *King of Kings* (1927), a film that drew some protests from Jewish organizations. To discuss the draft the West Coast Association of Producers set up a committee, composed incidentally of seven Jews and two Roman Catholics, appointed by that year's president, the Episcopalian oecumenicist, Cecil B. DeMille. Irving Thalberg chaired the committee (other members included Carl Laemmle Jr, B. P. Schulberg of Paramount, Sol Wurzel of Fox, Jack Warner and Joseph Schenck) and was later to describe the Code he helped formulate as 'his Bible' though a number of M-G-M movies, especially those featuring Jean Harlow, were to honour it in the breach. As Will Hays recalled the committee's deliberations, in his Rotarian rather than his pulpit style, 'the use or non-use of profanity was discussed – incidentally, with plenty of profanity – at many meetings and

until far into many a night'. The Code was formally adopted in
March 1930 by the West Coast Association[1] and the MPPDA
and immediately won the approval of the Vatican and the
Quebec Provincial Parliament which adopted it almost verbatim
as law. It was, however, something less than law in Hollywood
despite the lip service paid to it. Lapses from the Code were so
frequent in the early years of the depression – for reasons both
artistic and mercenary – that Hays continued to face heavy outside pressure, particularly from the Roman Catholic Church. He
arranged much publicized addresses to movie-makers by
prominent Catholic laymen such as A. H. Giannini, the
influential movie financier whose Bank of Italy had a special claim
on Hollywood consciences of whatever religious denomination.
But these did nothing to stem a tide which led to the formation
of the National Legion of Decency, a Catholic censorship body
and among the sharpest thorns in Hollywood's side for over thirty
years until its radical reform in the mid-sixties. (During this
period the Legion handed out moral classifications ranging from
A-I, which meant 'Morally Unobjectionable for General Patron-
age', to Class C for 'Condemned', and circulated its decisions
among Catholic communities throughout the world.)

To appease the Church it was therefore necessary to make the
Production Code mandatory and impose sanctions on its breach.
Accordingly in 1934 the ex-journalist Joseph I. Breen, the Irish-
American Catholic of Hays's Hollywood branch, was put in charge
of the Studio Relations Department which was re-named the
Production Code Administration, with power to withhold a certificate and Seal of Approval. A fine of 25,000 dollars was established for any member company releasing a film without the
Seal, but this was hardly necessary as relatively few cinemas (and
no large ones) were owned by non-MPPDA members or those
likely to exhibit a movie of which Hays disapproved, nor could

[1] The West Coast Association was established in 1924, and was later re-
entitled the Association of Motion Picture Producers Inc. (AMPP). Membership was confined to top studios and producers, and thus while there was a good
deal of overlap between it and the MPPDA, the AMPP was a smaller, more
select group. On important issues the two bodies invariably acted in concert.

79

an uncertified film be shown at any military or government establishment. The Code, one need hardly say, did not prevent good films from being made, but it did attempt to impose on movies a view of the world inconsistent to say the least with adult experience, and to rule out whole areas of life from film treatment. The idea of categorizing movies according to audience suitability (the system prevailing in Great Britain and most other countries) was until recently, and to a large extent continues to be, rejected by most movie moguls and American film-makers. Whatever the protestations to the contrary (freedom of speech, thin end of the wedge and so forth), the real reasons for this have been almost entirely commercial: to ensure that all films are acceptable to the lucrative teenage market and the family audience.

If the Code had been strictly adhered to, no film would in theory be capable of giving offence to any segment of the domestic or foreign market. In practice this has hardly proved the case. Equally at all stages of production, from deciding upon the feasibility of filming a book to the finished product, the Production Code Administration staff have been available to see how the work might be accommodated. And it must be said that ridiculous as many of its provisions were, the Code has been blamed for a good many faults whose source lay elsewhere.

The Code with its various amendments is a curious eight-page document that is at once dismaying and hilarious, repellent and fascinating. The Code begins with a preamble stating that producers recognize that 'though regarding motion pictures primarily as entertainment without any explicit purpose of teaching or propaganda, they know that the motion picture within its own field of entertainment may be directly responsible for spiritual or moral progress, for higher types of social life, and for much correct thinking'. There follows the statement of three general principles:

1. No picture shall be produced which will lower the moral standards of those who see it. Hence the sympathy of the audience shall never be thrown to the side of crime, wrong-doing, evil or sin.

2. Correct standards of life, subject only to the requirements of drama and entertainment, shall be presented.
3. Law, natural or human, shall not be ridiculed, nor shall sympathy be created for its violation.

This is succeeded by twelve sections of 'Particular Applications' – (i) Crimes Against the Law, (ii) Sex, (iii) Vulgarity, (iv) Obscenity, (v) Profanity, (vi) Costume, (vii) Dances, (viii) Religion, (ix) Location, (x) National Feelings, (xi) Titles, (xii) Repellent subjects – and three groups of additional Special Regulations on 'Crime in Motion Pictures', 'Costumes' and 'Cruelty to Animals'. The rest of the document, roughly half the length, is taken up with reasons supporting the preamble and reasons underlying the general principles and particular applications, and it concludes with the 1934 Resolution for uniform interpretation, indicating the Code Administration's right to see scripts and approve of completed films or films to be distributed by member companies.

Not all the Code's provisions are absurd; where reference is made to the handling of crime and the possibilities of imitation, they certainly are not, nor is it wrong to point out that an audience 'is most receptive of the emotions and ideals presented by their most popular stars.' The offensiveness of the Code lies in its tone, the comedy in its explicitness. For example, the entry on 'Profanity' actually lists twenty-eight prohibited words, e.g. 'gawd', 'hot (applied to a woman)', 'whore', and 'damn, hell (excepting where the use of the last two words shall be essential and required for portrayal, in proper historical context . . . or for the presentation in proper literary context of a Biblical or other quotation . . .).' The word 'bastard' in Laurence Olivier's *Henry V* raised objections in 1945 and even Shakespeare's name as screenwriter was insufficient to defend it.

Assumptions about 'accepted standards', good taste', right ideals', 'correct standards of life' and so on abound, and always the reference is to the tastes and standards of some ideal middle-western small town. This point is made clear in the reasons supporting the preamble:

Small communities, remote from sophistication and from the hardening process which often takes place in the ethical and moral standards of groups in larger cities, are easily and readily reached by any sort of film.

Will Hays must always have thought of his beloved Sullivan, Indiana, when he read that paragraph.

For general sanctimoniousness one can hardly better the notes on sex. Under particular applications, 'Sex perversion or any inference of it is forbidden' along with white slavery, miscegenation, abortion and scenes of 'actual child-birth', while 'Children's sex organs are never to be exposed'. In the 'Underlying reasons' section the Code points out the dangers of scenes of passion, especially on 'the young and the *criminal classes*' (I use the Code's italics throughout), warns of the 'limits of *pure love*' and then observes:

In the case of *impure love,* the love which society has always regarded as wrong and which has been banned by divine law, the following are important:

1   Impure love must not be presented as *attractive* and *beautiful.*
2   It must *not* be the subject of *comedy* or farce or treated as material for *laughter.*
3   It must not be presented in such a way as to *arouse passion* or morbid curiosity on the part of the audience.
4   It must not be made to seem *right and permissible.*
5   In general, it must *not* be *detailed* in method and manner.

Of the effects of the Code's attitude to sex, George Jean Nathan observed:

In the days before the Messrs Hays and Breen took over the morals of the movies, the screen frequently treated its male and female characters to a considerable sexual realism. But with the advent of the Hays-Breen censorship there came about a gradually cumulative change that, with negligible exception, has contrived to picture most characters in their amorous reactions to each other as practically indistinguishable from little children dressed up in their parents' clothes and playing house ... The theatre, often at its trashiest is forthright and honest in its approach, the screen often even at its best, is evasive and dishonest.[2]

[2]'The Movies in Love' in *The Entertainment of a Nation* (New York, Knopf, 1942).

The document's fascination with sex leads to the statement that 'The effect of *nudity or semi-nudity* upon the normal man or woman, and much more upon the young and upon immature persons, has been honestly recognized by all lawmakers and moralists'. It leads, too, to the note on 'Locations' reading, *in extenso*: 'The treatment of bedrooms must be governed by good taste and delicacy', followed later by the explanation: 'Certain places are so closely and thoroughly associated with sexual life and with sexual sin that their use must be carefully limited.' Also to be respected – virtually revered – are ministers of religion and all religious ceremony and the Flag, while 'The history, institutions, prominent people and citizenry of all nations shall be represented fairly'. The ultimate aim of it all is that 'if motion pictures consistently *hold up for admiration high types of characters* and present stories that will affect lives for the better they can become the most powerful natural force for the improvement of mankind'. Yet it need hardly be pointed out that if the Code was scrupulously followed, no possibility of social change would exist other than the strengthening of the status quo of the middleclass, middle-of-the-road American way of life.

One final point of the Code perhaps needs to be examined and that is the extent to which it is, or is not, a Catholic document, other, that is, than merely having been initiated by two Catholics. Some observers have detected Catholicism in the general moral character of the document as well as in such specific provisions as that on suicide:

Suicide, as a solution of problems occurring in the development of screen drama, is to be discouraged as morally questionable and as bad theatre – unless absolutely necessary for the development of the plot. It should never be justified or glorified or used to defeat the due process of law.

This provision led to the American re-make of Marcel Carné's *Le Jour se Lève – The Long Night* (1947) – concluding with the hero surrendering to the police instead of shooting himself. But more important evidence is found in the allusion to 'Natural Law' in the 'General Principles', which is essentially a Catholic concept and one little supported by non-Catholic jurists and not at all by social anthropologists. In the 'Underlying Reasons', this is explained thus:

> By *natural law* is understood the law which is written in the hearts of all mankind, the great underlying principles of right and justice dictated by conscience.

Of course, no film-maker was allowed to be dictated to by his conscience in the direction of socially subversive thought.

But this Code was for a mass, world-wide audience – for a public rhapsodized over by Elder Hays in his best pulpit manner when in 1936 a *Los Angeles Times* correspondent asked him 'What does the picture mean to you?'

> One stands on a high mountain and sees long lines of men, women and children moving slowly forward. They come from everywhere. They are rosy-cheeked girls from the farms, and their paler-faced sisters from the cities whose feet ache from long hours of standing behind bargain counters. There are plow boys, and sons of millionaires, and boys with the sallow cheeks of the tenements. There are old women with hands reddened and coarsened by work, and with eyes grown listless with long waiting. There are old men who hobble on crooked sticks, and children with the flash of the sun's gold in their hair and the happy laughter of innocence in their voices. There are the schoolboy and the savant, and the man of no learning at all. There are men and women of every race and every tongue, moving slowly forwards, seeking something, seeking, searching, yearning – asking for a place to dream. All about them is the roar of the cities, the confused, jangling noises of life that is hurried, rushed and propelled forward at a breathless speed. Every minute of every hour of every day they come – millions of them. And over and above them, and in front of them, attracting them on, offering that which they desire, are billions of flickering shadows – the motion pictures. Who shall estimate its importance? Who shall attempt to say what it means to the world?

Who indeed? If it was true that, as was often said, Louis B. Mayer was the greatest actor on the M-G-M lot, Hollywood certainly lost a potentially major screenwriter when Hays came to the movies as its czar instead of joining a script department.

The Production Code remained in effect for thirty-six years. For twenty of them (except for the year 1941 when he was in charge of production at RKO), Joseph Breen was its administrator. Breen even received a special Academy Award in 1953 for 'his conscientious, open-minded and dignified management of the Motion Picture Production Code'. His successor in 1954 was Geoffrey Shurlock, a mild-mannered, decisive, rather scholarly figure, who had been born in Liverpool in 1894, worked briefly at Paramount, and been on the Hays Office staff since 1932. In the second year of Shurlock's personal régime, considerable amendments were made to the Code without changing its general tenor. Nevertheless the alterations in interpretation enabled Otto Preminger to return and obtain a certificate for *The Moon is Blue* ten years after Joe Breen had refused to license it. Preminger, who (as we shall later see) was among the first to defy the Hollywood black-list, challenged Breen by a literal adaptation of a fairly innocuous Broadway sex comedy that happened to use proscribed terms like 'professional virgin' and so on. Released without a certificate, the movie showed a handsome profit, and while it might have caused some consternation in the Hays (or rather now the Johnston) Office, the general public reaction was one of amusement at the succession of mildly *risqué* jokes, and disappointment at the talkative movie's failure to live up to its controversial reputation. A decade after its initial release, *The Moon is Blue* presented Geoffrey Shurlock with no serious problems.

Gradually eroded, open to widely differing interpretation, almost universally despised, the Code came to an end in 1966, the year that Jack Valenti quit the White House to become President of the MPAA; the sharp, articulate, liberal Texan was very different from the folksy, conservative middle-westerner who forty-five years earlier – in 1921, the year Valenti was born – had left President Harding's cabinet upon receipt of the founding moguls' round robin. On 20 September 1966 a 'New Code of Self Regulation' for production, advertising and titles, approved by the MPAA, became effective. This New Code differed greatly from its predecessor, and with it Hollywood came abreast of contemporary American and international tendencies. Not that the four-page document was without its rhetoric, but the prevailing tone was urban, permissive, post-Freudian, reasonable, unembattled. 'This revised Code,' it began, 'is designed to keep in closer harmony with the mores, the culture, the moral sense and the expectations of our society', and two objects were proposed: '1. To encourage artistic expression by expanding creative freedom; 2. To assure that the freedom which encourages the artist remains responsible and sensitive to the standards of the larger society.'

'Censorship is an odious enterprise', the Declaration of Principles goes on. 'We oppose censorship and classification-by-law (or whatever name or guise these restrictions go under) because they are alien to the American tradition of freedom.' Casting aside Natural Law, the New Code opts for a 'test of self-restraint' and 'the rule of reason' which must govern the treatment of a subject for the screen – 'the Seal of the MPAA on a film means that the picture has met the test of self-regulation'. Taking a very different view of America from the committee appointed by Cecil B. DeMille in 1930, the MPAA now asserts that 'We believe in and pledge our support to the deep and fundamental values in a democratic society: Freedom of choice ... The right of creative men to achieve artistic excellence ... The role of the parent as the arbiter of the family's conduct'.

The Code then sets out a list of 'Standards for Production'. The first of these is that 'The basic dignity and value of human life shall be respected and upheld' while 'Evil, sin, crime and wrong-doing shall not be justified'. As to criminal and anti-social activities 'special restraint' must be observed when 'minors participate or are involved', and 'no detailed or protracted acts of brutality, cruelty, physical violence, torture or abuse' shall be countenanced. Likewise in the matter of speech, physical exposure and sexual aberration, the key words are 'restraint' and 'no undue'. The lists of prohibited terms have been abandoned, replaced by admonitions such as that 'words, or symbols contemptuous of racial, religious or national groups, shall not be used so as to incite bigotry or hatred'. The standards for advertising insist upon no 'cumulative over-emphasis on sex, crime, violence and brutality', that censorship disputes should 'not be exploited or capitalized upon', and that the character of a movie must not be misrepresented. There is also appended at the end the note that the Code Administrators may recommend that the film be advertised as 'Suggested for Maturer Audiences' and consequently left to parental arbitration. Nowhere in the document are to be found the vague, challengeable assumptions or the stabbing italics that punctuated and punctured the old Hays Office Code.

From the point of view of those who made pictures, as well as that large minority who regard the cinema as a great art form and a medium for the expression of ideas and dissemination of information, the fundamental criticism of Hays is that he was a fixer, a conciliator, and at heart on the side of the reactionary opposition. During his 1936 visit to Rome to negotiate with Mussolini, he took very seriously the warning given him by the Pope of a concerted Communist scheme to infiltrate the world movie industry. He thus attempted to imbue Hollywood with a premature Red scare, and as special adviser to the MPPDA for a five-year period after his retirement in 1945 his counsel was to root out every possible suspect from Hollywood. Hays's method was never to stand up and answer back when a critical issue arose, but to seek a compromise or smooth things over, even though he himself had no financial stake in the business. In some cases this practice was wise – as it surely was when in 1933 he went to Washington to talk the newly-elected President Roosevelt out of a federal scheme to control the industry. It is a moot point as to whether Hays acted wisely the following year in making a personal approach to the rabble-rousing 'Radio Priest' Father Coughlin to dissuade him from going on the air to denounce what he regarded as a dangerous Jewish monoply of the film business. Although the mission succeeded, an open confrontation might have been more desirable.

One would not claim that Hays was lacking in moral courage; rather that it was not in his nature and training to stand up for the political or artistic rights of those with whom he disagreed against those with whom he sided. In this unfortunately he had the backing of the moguls whose over-riding interest was in protecting and enlarging their investment. He served them well. But such progress as Hollywood made in advancing the medium towards some kind of maturity was achieved, if not actually despite him, certainly without his encouragement. Had the film-makers themselves been prepared to follow his lead the movies would have remained in the kindergarten. The limitations of Hays's conception of the cinema's role is perhaps most clearly to be found in his own tribute of the mid-thirties:

No medium has contributed more than the films to the mainten-ance of the national morale during a period featured by revolutions, riot and political turmoil in other countries. It has been the mission of the screen, without ignoring the serious social problems of the day, to reflect aspiration, achievement, optimism and kindly humour in its entertainment. Historians of the future will not ignore the interesting and significant fact that the movies literally laughed the big bad wolf of depression out of the public.

Seven years before Hays came to office, the United States Supreme Court upheld a mid-western censorship board's auth-ority with these words (Mutual Film Corporation *v.* Industrial Commission, 236 U.S. 1915):

It cannot be put out of view that the exhibition of moving pictures is a business pure and simple, originated and conducted for profit, like other spectacles, not to be regarded, nor intended to be regarded by the Ohio Constitution, we think, as part of the process of the country or as organs of public opinion.

Seven years after Hays's retirement, the Supreme Court rejected its own earlier decision in over-ruling the New York censors who had attempted to prevent the exhibition of the Italian movie *The Miracle* on the grounds that the movie was 'sacrilegious'. In its historic finding that films were protected by the First and Fourteenth Amendments, the Court stated on Monday, 19 May 1952:

It cannot be doubted that motion pictures are a significant medium for the communication of ideas. They may affect public attitudes and behaviour in a variety of ways, ranging from direct espousal of a political or a social doctrine to the subtle shaping of thought which characterises all artistic expression. The importance of motion pictures as an organ of public opinion is not lessened by the fact that they are designed to entertain as well as to inform . . .

It is urged that motion pictures do not fall within the First Amendment's aegis because their production, distribution and exhibition is a large-scale business conducted for private profit. We can not agree. That books, newspapers and magazines are published and sold for profit does not prevent them from being a form of expression whose liberty is safeguarded by the First Amendment.

We fail to see why operation for profit should have any different effect in the case of motion pictures.

It is further urged that motion pictures possess a greater capacity for evil, particularly among the youth of the community, than other modes of expression. Even if one were to accept this hypothesis, it does not follow that motion pictures should be disqualified from First Amendment protection. If there be capacity for evil it may be relevant in determining the permissible scope of community control, but it does not authorise substantially unbridled censorship such as we have here.

For the foregoing reasons, we conclude that expression by means of motion pictures is included within the free speech and free press guarantee of the First and Fourteenth Amendments.

7

THE OUTSIDERS

There's only one thing sure about my boy Bill.
I've been watching him and notice that when he
wants cake, he wants cake, and he wants it now,
and I notice that after a while he gets the cake.

Senator George Hearst

In its years of greatness, and even in its years of decline, Hollywood attracted the attention of the world and the personal in-
spection of its most illustrious and notorious citizens. George
Bernard Shaw dropped in for a visit, the exiled Thomas Mann
settled in the vicinity (and was by no means reluctant to accept
an invitation to meet little Shirley Temple); America's presidents
were guests at the studios; royalty always included the movie
colony in their itineraries; and as late as 1959 Nikita Khrush-
chev's American tour would have been incomplete without a stop-
over there, as would that of Princess Margaret and Lord Snowdon
six years later. But among the mighty and the mountebanks who
graced Hollywood with their presence no trio of outsiders took a
closer interest in the business or made a greater impact than
William Randolph Hearst, Joseph Kennedy and Howard Hughes,
three of the most extraordinary Americans of the century. All
three considered themselves a cut above the moguls, and with
good reason, but all three wanted to be moguls themselves. These
tall ruthless teetotallers, who refrained from the gambling tables
as assiduously as they took chances in business, came from backgrounds alien both to the pioneers and to Will Hays. To the
industry's czar the press lord Hearst and the Catholic family man
Kennedy were welcome; Hughes, however, was an intermittent
nuisance to him and the studio moguls for thirty years.

Hearst came to Hollywood with his mistress Marion Davies
to the furtherance of whose career his vast newspaper chain and
Cosmopolitan Film company were dedicated. By the early twen-

ties, his hopes of achieving the presidency were over, and this return to his native California as his sixtieth birthday approached was a partial retreat from public life to a place where he could indulge his fantasies in the creation of his dream palace, San Simeon, where he installed his fairy princess while his wife remained on the East Coast. He did not altogether abandon politics; indeed he was a key figure in the election of Franklin Roosevelt, and his money and influence made him someone to be courted as much by Hitler or Churchill as by Hollywood. Moreover as a man who had befriended the immigrant underdog at the turn of the century, had started wars, lived with a total disregard for convention and public opinion, and built an inherited fortune into one of America's greatest empires, Hearst was a legendary figure, an epic hero of his age. Merely to be in his presence was an honour, and to be regularly his guest was the apogee of public acceptance and, for movie tycoons, a rich compensation for a lifetime of petty slights. And unlike most Americans of his age and background, Hearst was wholly untainted by anti-semitism, despite the fact that his reactionary politics often brought him semi-fascist, anti-semitic allies. Whatever he did was news (not only in his own journals), and to mix with Hearst was to be drawn into the magic circle of international society. What did it matter that his pictures consistently lost money for Hearst and those associated with him? After all, the incalculable value of the publicity he could hand out, the contacts he could provide, and his personal company more than made up for any pecuniary loss. So, among others, thought Louis Mayer who was only too happy to make Cosmopolitan at home on the M-G-M lot, to pay Miss Davies 10,000 dollars a week and have her so-called bungalow erected at Culver City after the absorption of Goldwyn films which had previously handled Hearst's productions. More than anyone else Hearst was responsible for building up Mayer outside the industry; the two held almost identical views on public morality (the Hearst press had led the sensational campaign against the hapless Fatty Arbuckle), all-Americanism, and right-wing politics – though in his youth Hearst had been considered a socialist. Their mutual admiration survived over the years a difference of opinion concerning the merits of Herbert Hoover, and the departure in the mid-thirties of Cosmopolitan from M-G-M when Mayer supported Irving Thalberg's refusal to cast Marion Davies as Elizabeth Barrett. The part in *The Barretts of Wimpole Street* went to Thalberg's wife Norma Shearer (who for a while found herself on the Hearst newspapers' blacklist) and Miss Davies went to Warner Brothers along with her fourteen-room bungalow which was cut into sections and dragged across town on rollers. Warners were pleased to handle Miss Davies's pictures for the few years that remained of her career. Jack Warner was even to claim, in the face of certain evidence to the contrary, that the films actually showed a profit.

Louis B. Mayer, however, never went quite that far. In the 'twenties he was confronted by a sales convention more than a little surprised that the studio was asking its representatives to sell such unwelcome material as Cosmopolitan generally produced. Mayer spoke of Miss Davies's personal attraction (which was undoubted, but owing to Hearst's extraordinary whim she was being forced into one ludicrously expensive fairy-tale after the other instead of the light comedies to which she was better suited); he ran through the benefits of Hearst publicity to the studio and then gave the bewildered gathering a highly coloured Horatio Alger-style biography of his hero and his hero's father, the self-made multi-millionaire, Senator George Hearst. Whipping himself up into one of the histrionic frenzies for which he was famous, Mayer concluded, as reported by his biographer Bosley Crowther: 'This is what I want to impress upon you gentlemen. This is the spirit that has made America great. We live in a land of opportunity! God bless America!' His audience was suitably stunned.

Fifteen years later Mayer weighed in again on behalf of Hearst, and this time entirely altruistically. When he heard that in the RKO film *Citizen Kane* (1941) Orson Welles had drawn an identifiable portrait of the press lord, he got Nick Schenck to approach RKO president George Schaefer with an 800,000 dollar offer to scrap the movie. The proposal was turned down and as a result a rumour that the Roman Catholic Schaefer was an anti-semite began to move around Hollywood. The rumour was traced back to Mayer. So too was a conspiracy to prevent the picture from being widely shown after it had gained excellent reviews (other than in the Hearst press where *Kane* was ignored and Welles blacklisted). Threatened legal action resulted in the Warner Brothers accepting it for distribution in their cinemas, but the picture never received the opportunities it so manifestly deserved. Hearst himself it seems was less upset than his friends and lieutenants; his real worry was the pain that had been caused to Miss Davies ('grotesque', she called the picture) who emerged in a more pathetic light than he did. During his virtual retirement in the war years he had a copy of it in his private cinema. In retrospect *Citizen Kane*, among the best films to come from Hollywood and always named in lists of the ten best pictures ever made, stands ironically as Hearst's abiding contribution to the cinema.

Hollywood was bound up with the twilight dreams of Hearst's career, with the cinema as the only means of realizing his Camelot, the inexpressible, almost Arthurian world which he longed to rule with Marion Davies as his queen; and also with the unreserved adulation in which he basked as the cynosure of Hollywood social life. The ageing giant teddy bear, whom Miss Davies called 'Pops', kidded himself he was in the business for money, but only when his money began to run out elsewhere did he abandon it. For there was both a childish and a child-like side to Hearst that underlay his ruthlessness and ambition. He behaved like a spoilt kid very often and his obsession with collecting things he could never use was childish. Like most of the moguls, too, he was endlessly fascinated by practical jokes, and it was indeed for one such elaborately planned prank that he was thrown out of Harvard; practical jokers often seem to be people who have never quite come to terms with the adult world and are constantly attempting to assuage their unease by exposing its pomposities. But more than that, he had a child's fascination with exploring things, and his first interest in the cinema was directing his own, often quite elaborate home movies, and his romantic adolescent dreams dictated the adult pursuits he cloaked under cover of business. This quality it was that Orson Welles seized on as the clue to Hearst's character and used to determine the formal structure of *Citizen Kane*.

Joseph Kennedy, on the other hand, had no time for the moguls and no interest in the business other than the quick profit. If one thinks of Hearst as never quite growing up, one finds it equally hard to think of Kennedy as ever having been young and carefree. The tall, thin, red-haired Bostonian had surveyed the 'twenties scene coolly, and observed this plum tree waiting to be shaken with even greater and more scientific vigour than anyone had previously attempted. He was quite as ruthless as the young Hearst had been, and unhandicapped by the press lord's quixotic qualities. Kennedy was, in the words of a Harvard contemporary, 'the kind of guy, who, if he wanted something badly enough, would get it, and he didn't care how he got it. He'd run right over anybody.' Coming from an Irish immigrant background he understood the moguls. His own grandfather was a failed immigrant who had suffered exclusion and died a broken man at the age of thirty-five. As a child Joe used to make a little pocket money lighting fires on the Sabbath and feast days in the homes of Boston's orthodox Jewish community; from his earliest days he had few pursuits that were not money-making. But he had little sympathy for the moguls and their lack of business efficiency. Kennedy at twenty-five had become America's youngest bank president (of admittedly one of the country's smallest banks), had more or less achieved his long-standing ambition to make his first million by the age of thirty-five, and when in 1926 he entered the movie industry he told a colleague: 'Look at that bunch of pants pressers in Hollywood making themselves millionaires. I could take the whole business away from them.' Unlike other financiers who invested and dictated policy through boardroom nominees, Kennedy threw himself into the movies with total dedication through his company, the Film Booking Office of America, wheeling and dealing twenty-four hours a day between New York and Hollywood. 'A banker! A banker? I thought this business was just for furriers,' said Marcus Loew when he heard of Kennedy's incursion.

Like Hearst, Kennedy made a minimal contribution to the art of the cinema. His university and Boston background had already given him a certain prestige; and the ultimate national estime he sought was to be derived from a financial empire that would form a basis for his own political career and serve as a launching pad for the fourth generation of Irish exiles, his formidable brood of sons whom he was rearing to be as harshly competitive as himself. Cheap money-making films were his line, aimed at the undemanding patrons of small-town movie houses. (The teen-age Joe Kennedy Jr and the eleven-year-old John F. were used by their father as an audience sounding board for his projects.) But his real business was in building up his newly acquired company, bringing it together with other exhibition and production corporations and getting out with a quick killing. And God help anyone who stood in his way. The chief of the Keith-Albee theatre circuit, for instance, thought he was a trusted partner until the morning he came into the office after joining up with Kennedy to be told: 'Didn't you know, Ed? You're washed up. You're through.' Such was the elevating example of artistic quality and business ethics that the Harvard-educated tycoon set to the industry.

This didn't worry Will Hays too much. He was able to ignore such backroom strife or accept it as normal conduct. What mattered to him was to be head of an industry that could attract such a sound business- and family-man. And Kennedy amply repaid the moguls by giving them a moment of real glory for which they would be forever grateful. In 1927 Kennedy persuaded the Harvard Business School to recognize the importance of the country's fourth largest industry by staging a series of lectures for second year students enrolled in the school's business policy course. He was not entirely disinterested; such lectures would raise his own prestige, benefit investment by improving the image of the industry into which he had barged only a few months previously, and provide him with a little personal reassurance. So in March and April 1927 a string of moguls went to Harvard to speak on every aspect of the movies; later that year Kennedy published the texts and transcripts of the subsequent discussions as a book edited by himself. Naturally Kennedy kicked off the series in person, taking it upon himself to present the industry and its leaders, whose professional peer he thus by implication became, to the Ivy League audience. Prophetically in the course of the inaugural lecture he dropped a hint that the industry was 'on the eve of great consolidations', and made a deliberate employment pitch to his young listeners:

... it may be worth your while to consider why, in view of its splendid opportunities, relatively few college men are in it. I do not mind telling you that there are desirable places in the industry which college men could fill. It has reached a stage of development at which it really needs the services of men like yourselves, men trained to analyse problems and build up solutions on the basis of accurate knowledge and approved mercantile methods.

Kennedy was followed by one of the rare college men in the industry, Will Hays, the distinguished graduate of Wabash College, Crawfordsville, Indiana, known while 'the czar' was a student there as 'the Athens of the Midwest', though it seems scarcely likely that the three hundred Harvard men gathered in the Baker Memorial Hall would have been much impressed by this epithet. Hays, as was his wont and indeed his job, spoke of the moguls that were to lecture later in the series in rather more fulsome terms than Kennedy had done:

These men who will speak to you realise that they are responsible custodians not only of one of the greatest industries of the world, but of a most potent instrument for moral influence, inspiration and education and of the most universal medium of art that the world has ever known...

From the business stand-point, the motion picture industry has settled down and is operating along the sound, common-sense lines which govern other American industries. The early, reckless extravagance is no more. Much waste of time and effort has been eliminated. It is no longer the 'motion picture game'; it is the 'motion picture business'.

Hays went on to boast, somewhat ironically in the circumstances, of the success of the informal 'Hays formula' for self-censorship, and how as a result of circulating the companies with information about undesirable material 'more than a hundred and fifty books and plays, including some of the best sellers and stage successes, have thus been kept off the screen'. This must have gone down very well with an audience of bright young men in Boston. He also told the students about 'trade following the film' and stressed the importance of cinematic diplomats like himself. He instanced the movie *The Eternal City* and how he had 'called the Italian ambassador, Signor Caetani, on the telephone, and told him we want to make this correctly from Italy's point of view'. With the advice of the ambassador, 'a most distinguished man, who ... marched beside Mussolini in a black shirt on Rome', Hays proudly claimed that 'we made a picture thoroughly sympathetic and pleasing to Italy and told a true story of things as they are'.

Hays was followed by such unlettered luminaries as Adolph Zukor, Jesse Lasky, Cecil B. DeMille, Sidney Kent, Robert Cochrane, Harry Warner, William Fox and Marcus Loew, as well as the ex-nickelodeon pianist and Northwestern University alumnus Sam Katz. 'Twenty years ago,' said Fox, 'to have expected to have Harvard agree to have someone meet with its students and tell them something about motion pictures would have been a sacrilege.' (Fox had once warned his two children: 'Don't tell your friends your father is in the cinema business. It isn't quite respectable.') And the richest of them all, Marcus Loew, was even more affected: 'I cannot begin to tell you how it impresses me, coming to a great college such as this to deliver a lecture, when I have never even seen the inside of one before.' Loew had actually left his sick bed to come up to Cambridge to deliver his talk; before the lectures were published in book form that autumn, he was dead.

Having given the tycoons this privileged glimpse of his alma mater, Kennedy did not long remain among them. A series of mergers followed during which he received a colossal salary and advisory fees; he had learnt incidentally from the tycoons the value of taking a weekly salary rather than an annual one. Then, the foundations of RKO laid, Kennedy hung on long enough to see his stock fall and as sharply rise again to new peaks, before he sold out and disappeared. Thirty-two months in the movies had made him a multi-millionaire. For a short while thereafter he carried on as consultant and financier to Miss Gloria Swanson during her career as producer of her own pictures, being instrumental in suppressing her first independent feature film, Erich von Stroheim's *Queen Kelly,* and thus putting the penultimate nail in the director's coffin. No one was particularly worried. Kennedy's claim that he took a large personal loss as the result of this decision is not borne out by Miss Swanson who testifies that she repaid every penny with interest from the profits of her subsequent pictures.

Joseph Kennedy is not an easy man to like though he is not actually difficult to understand. The lengthy, contradictory career of Hearst makes him an impossible man to grasp in his entirety: his *New York Times* obituary ran to twenty thousand words. But no one has even begun to explain Howard Hughes, unless the purpose of his life has been to create an impenetrable mystery, a theory that has been seriously advanced. In 1924, at an age when Hearst and Kennedy were still Harvard undergraduates, Hughes had inherited his father's commercial empire, and with a small part of the proceeds came to Hollywood to set up as an independent producer. The moguls took the thin, shy, slightly deaf six-foot-three Texan for a wealthy innocent, ready to be duped. He probably never got over this, and certainly he must have despised them as much as he loathed the conventional morality of Will Hays. His formal education was limited by his own restlessness. He was prepared for Harvard, but after the death of his mother when he was seventeen he had gone off to California with his father who liked the Hollywood crowd. He attended some courses at the Californian Institute of Technology and then enrolled at Texas' Rice Institute which he left after one term, on his father's death. That he had inherited his father's drive along with his mechanical aptitude was shown when he persuaded a judge to let him take over the Hughes Tool Company immediately, instead of waiting until he was twenty-one; an inherited ruthlessness showed itself the same year when on a trans-Atlantic steamer he obtained the best cabin by bribing the captain to eject the distinguished physician who had reserved it. Like Hearst and Kennedy, he discovered at an early age that with money you can buy almost anything or anybody, a belief that the subsequent events of his life did little to weaken.

He learnt the movie business the hard way – by stripping down a camera and putting it together again, and by producing a disastrous movie at great expense, then scrapping it. His second film showed a reasonable return, and his third won an Oscar as the year's best comedy in the first roster of Academy Awards in 1928. He was still only twenty-two. Next he stunned the movie colony with *Hell's Angels,* the violent, sexy first-world-war flying extravaganza which he directed himself. He worked on it for over two years, doubling the cost to four million dollars by largely re-shooting it as a sound picture. During this long, hectic period his neglected wife left him, he sold his chain of movie houses to raise more money, and eventually earned eight million dollars from the picture. His interest in aviation grew while making *Hell's Angels* and was to compete with films for his attention for over thirty years. Several flops followed before he hit the jackpot with *The Front Page* (1931) and *Scarface* (1932), which he saw as the gangster film to end them all. Over *Scarface* he fought a running battle with Will Hays, first making some cuts that the czar suggested, and then restoring them after a successful legal action against the New York Board of Censors which had refused to grant him a certificate. He shook the authority of the Hays organization then as he was to do fifteen years later with *The Outlaw.*

Around this time Hughes deliberately changed his life style, dressing like a tramp and growing increasingly eccentric. He walked out on Hollywood and worked under a pseudonym as an airline pilot, before re-emerging in the mid-thirties to start his Hughes Aircraft Company and establish the first of a series of flying speed records for transcontinental and round-the-world flights. Despite his hatred of publicity he still kept company with film stars and starlets, whom he accompanied to all the leading night-clubs. At times he was rumoured to be engaged to, among others, Katherine Hepburn, Lana Turner, Ginger Rogers and

Olivia de Havilland. Yet he still shunned interviews, conducted his business from all-night diners, worked mainly on public phones, was capable of parking a car and forgetting where he left it, and on one occasion was picked up in a midwestern town as a vagrant. However, while he switched around from one interest to the other, living a chaotic, apparently disorganized life, the ever more complicated strands of his empire were kept together by his brilliant accountant Noah Dietrich who had been with him since 1925.

A national hero as an aviator, and with the war to become one of the nation's biggest defence (and later aerospace) contractors, Hughes decided to return to the movies in 1939. He mentioned his decision to David Selznick's press agent, Russell Birdwell, after the première of *Gone With the Wind*. One suspects that the success of Selznick had spurred the competitive Hughes into challenging the pre-eminence of Hollywood's Number One genius. The result was *The Outlaw* which Hughes intended as the ultimate in Westerns in the same way that *Scarface* aimed to be the definitive gangster picture. There was no love for Hughes in Hollywood and the immediate response of the industry was M-G-M's rushing out its own version of *Billy the Kid* to steal Hughes's thunder. It was not just that they had agreed that Hughes was a disgrace to the industry, a public rocker of the boat, but they disapproved of his eccentric behaviour, his communion with the likes of Errol Flynn and the ease with which he threw writs around. Howard Hawks was first assigned to direct *The Outlaw*, but soon Hughes himself took over the direction of the unknown chiropodist's assistant Jane Russell, for whose now legendary bosom he designed a special brassiere on 'a very simple engineering principle'. Shooting went on intermittently for two years with Hughes filming the interior sequences at night and overseeing his factory's war work by day. A battle with Hays followed once more; now Hays was in a stronger position and over a hundred changes were demanded and made. Despite this, the film was advertised on its San Francisco opening as 'The picture they couldn't stop' in a publicity campaign of almost unparalleled lubricity (e.g. 'How'd you like to tussle with Russell?') devised personally by the director. The movie did poorly until a sustained attempt by Hughes and his press agent to have the film banned reached its climax in the cinema manager's arrest. He was acquitted after a sensational trial; the public flocked in; Hughes withdrew the picture. Not until 1946 did he finally release it after a further sensational campaign. *The Outlaw* broke box-office records everywhere.

Meanwhile the war had ended, Hughes was inestimable millions richer, and had survived a crash landing while testing the prototype of a new 400 m.p.h. fighter. The papers had his obituaries set up in type and his heroic recovery from appalling injuries (he designed a new hospital bed while convalescing) went some way towards mitigating the disapprobation that *The Outlaw* had brought him. To celebrate his return to active life he proceeded to turn his airline companies into the vast Trans-World Airlines organization and then acquired the RKO Radio film company. At this time (1947) he made one of his few public appearances when called before a Senate Committee investigating defence contracts. Hughes faced the brow-beating chairman of the committee with patrician disdain. 'As for me,' he told him, 'I have been called capricious, a playboy, eccentric, but I don't believe I have the reputation of a liar. I think my reputation in that respect meets what most Texans consider important.' He gave a cool, modestly impressive performance of calculated diffidence and turned up for the hearings in his customary rumpled clothing. After successfully answering all the charges, he emerged to be greeted by a spontaneous nation-wide campaign to have him run for president. The brief experience of the limelight, however, had been enough and he rapidly retreated from the embarrassing invitations to play a permanent role in American public life.

RKO, never a happy company, was even unhappier under Hughes, who gave it too little of his time. Most of his energy was now taken up by the burgeoning electronics industry. His head of production Dore Schary left after disagreements to join M-G-M, and a variety of people were brought in to run production units, most notably the team of Jerry Wald and Norman Krasna.

Hughes appointed Noah Dietrich Chairman of the Board and himself took the title 'Managing Director – Production'. But he rarely went near the studio. The company, said Hughes, was 'a damned nuisance; it represents 15 per cent of my business and takes 85 per cent of my time'. Long-time contract stars and newly signed European performers like Gina Lollobrigida and Jean Simmons grew restless with inactivity and neglect. The studio made some good movies over the years, but generally it was in a sick way and lacking in strong guidance.

Having successfully competed with the star-making moguls by creating the reputations of Jean Harlow in *Hell's Angels* and Jane Russell in *The Outlaw*, Hughes had set out immediately after the war, before buying RKO, to launch the career of Faith Domergue. He had acquired her services in the first year of the war from Warner Brothers, who were grooming the then fifteen-year-old actress for possible stardom under a seven-year contract. Hughes had kept her hanging around for four years, always with the promise that a new movie company he was starting with Preston Sturges would find a vehicle for her. Not until 1946 did shooting start upon her first picture, a torrid adaptation from Prosper Merimée called *Vendetta*, which she had chosen herself from a pile of possible scripts. Several million dollars and the efforts of half-a-dozen directors were expended, not to mention reels and reels of film scrapped after sporadic shooting, before in 1950 an eighty-four minute mouse of a movie was released by RKO. *Vendetta* did not make the undoubtedly attractive but not especially talented Miss Domergue a star. It certainly exacerbated Hughes's already frustrated condition.

Hughes's chief interest in RKO came during the black-listing period. Like the Red-scare artist Hearst and the Joseph McCarthy-supporter Kennedy, he had the anti-communist virus in as virulent a form as any of Hollywood's worst right-wingers. (His uncle, the ageing screenwriter Rupert Hughes, was a founder-member of the Motion Picture Alliance for the Preservation of American Ideals and one of the first 'friendly witnesses' to testify on communist infiltration before the House Un-American Activities Committee.) Hughes saw anyone who stood in his way,

26 Press lord and would-be movie tycoon William Randolph Hearst, surrounded by his art treasures, playing a lonely game of Patience at his Californian retreat, San Simeon. This famous portrait by Dr Salomon bears a striking resemblance to stills from Orson Welles's *Citizen Kane*.

Jack L. Warner as he testified yesterday

Louis B. Mayer (right) talking to Eric Johnston

27 Two of the friendly witnesses who visited Washington in 1947 to protest their patriotism and assure the nation that at Warner Brothers and M-G-M at least all left-wing artists were kept under constant surveillance. The massive press coverage that glamorous star witnesses attracted to these initial hearings helped promote the post-war Red Scare and prepared the way for a decade of black-listing and suspicion.

28 Howard Hughes, multi-millionaire genius and recluse, who opposed his fellow movie moguls in practically everything but the smoking out of alleged subversives in which activity he took a leading part.

29 Joseph P. Kennedy, the Boston banker turned film tycoon turned diplomat, pictured in 1938 when he took up his appointment as US Ambassador to the Court of St James. 'A banker! A banker? I thought this business was just for furriers,' said Marcus Loew.

30 Former President of the United States, Calvin Coolidge (left), visits the M-G-M studio and prepares to go before the microphones with Republican activist Louis B. Mayer, whose entrée to the White House during the administrations of Coolidge and Herbert Hoover proved immensely advantageous.

31 A welcome to Hollywood for President Harding's ex-Postmaster General, Will Hays, appointed the industry's 'Czar' in 1922 to put the film world's rickety house in order. Hays is shaking hands with producer Jesse Lasky, who is wearing his customary pince-nez and stiff collar. At left is Cecil B. DeMille in his traditional 'shooting' outfit.

32 Jack L. Warner (left) with the Austrian theatre director Max Reinhardt (centre), who co-directed his only sound movie *A Midsummer Night's Dream* for Warner Brothers in 1935, and William Randolph Hearst, whose Cosmopolitan Films moved in 1934 from M-G-M to Warner Brothers' Burbank studio. To commemorate *A Midsummer Night's Dream* a special medallion was struck with the profiles of Shakespeare and Reinhardt to left and right and the three Warner Brothers in the middle.

33 The 'Czar' Will Hays presents an album of photographs to the industry's elder statesman, Adolph Zukor. Hays's large ears, here prominently displayed, together with his Indiana background, caused him to be dubbed 'the Hoosier Clark Gable', a sobriquet he greatly cherished.

whether it was the armed forces with whom he had contracts or employees in his aircraft firm who wanted a greater say in administration, as being communist-influenced. With the studio he could strike harder. He shut down RKO for three months while staff loyalty was investigated. He tried to prevent Chaplin's *Limelight* from being shown in any RKO cinema. To the Hollywood branch of the American Legion he said:

In spite of all the movement to whitewash the industry, to say that there is no Red Influence in Hollywood, to sweep this matter under the carpet and hide it and pretend that it does not exist, in spite of that there is a substantial number of people in the motion picture industry who follow the Communist party line.

One is tempted to conjecture that Hughes was taking out on the RKO, of which he once said 'I need it like I need the plague', the more bitter frustrations engendered by his other enterprises. Losing millions a year at RKO, Hughes was becoming the laughing stock of Hollywood; the moguls were having their revenge at last. In the mid-fifties, in a complex deal, Hughes rid himself of RKO, and as a film-making entity it went out of existence, the old movies going to television and the studio passing into the hands of a television producing company. At the same time he divorced Hughes Aircraft from Hughes Tool, and set up the Howard Hughes Medical Institute to operate with the former's profits.

Hughes was now out of movies for good, as he was also out of active control of his aircraft company and the TWA airline; he later sold his stock in the latter for 546.5 million dollars. With his ex-movie star wife, the beautiful Jean Peters (whom he married in 1957, thus keeping his word that he would never remarry until over the age of fifty), Hughes lived in unbreachable seclusion in the exclusive Bel Air neighbourhood of north Los Angeles, before shifting his centre of activity to Las Vegas. There, worth something in excess of two thousand million dollars, he proceeded methodically to take possession of the city and environs. In this activity, according to current reports, he is still engaged, working from a closely guarded base in the Desert Inn, one of a string of casinos that this non-gambling, non-smoking teetotaller now improbably owns. It is said that the 30,000 acres of land outside Las Vegas that he has purchased is earmarked for use as a vast airport to receive supersonic jets bringing passengers to the entire West Coast. That he might return to Hollywood at the age of sixty-three is by no means impossible. He has returned before, and on several occasions his name has inevitably been linked to apparent takeover bids, including a recent one for M-G-M. But there is no real challenge awaiting him there any longer, no moguls worth mocking or bombarding with writs, no Will Hays to provoke into puritanical wrath, no boy geniuses left to match his wits against. Television, however, has attracted him (he already owns a Las Vegas station) and in the summer of 1968 he made an attempt to purchase a controlling interest in the ABC television network, which was blocked, partly by ABC executives and partly by the Federal Communications Commission's warning that this would put him over the maximum five stations anyone is allowed to own, and by the Commission's announcement that it would hold public hearings on the bid. 'The best way to defeat Hughes,' *Time* commented, 'seems to be to threaten him with the necessity of appearing in public.'

Nowadays Hughes is, in the phrase of *Time*'s stable-mate *Fortune,* 'The Spook of American Capitalism'. Like the aged Hearst before him and the partially paralysed Joseph Kennedy still, it is only when his name occasionally appears in the press that the public is reminded that this once celebrated figure remains among the living. His perceptive and fair-minded biographer John Keats was reminded, however, when two years ago Hughes sought unsuccessfully to prevent the publication of a biographical study. As Keats had observed: 'Hughes is quite capable of ruining a man who tries to run him down. Few men, however mighty, take the risk.'

8

AMERICANS AND UN-AMERICANS

I'm an American and not a Jew.
David O. Selznick

One widely accepted theory for the preponderance of Jews among the film pioneers has always been that of Jewish internationalism, though as I have indicated it is not a view I share. In the first important history of the cinema, *A Million and One Nights* (1926), Terry Ramsaye writes:

It is not an accident but rather a phase of screen evolution which finds the American motion picture industry, and therefore the screens of the world, administered rather largely by our best and most facile internationalists, the Jews, with those of Russian extraction slightly predominant over the Germans.

There is little more than a grain of truth in this argument. The movie pioneers were no better equipped for the task of overseas expansion than anyone else engaged in American industrial imperialism. Economic necessity was the force behind the international-mindedness of the movie business. In fact the Hollywood tycoons were intensely nationalistic, if in a confused and indiscriminate way, and this put a mark upon their movies.

Each and every one was committed to the idea of being American. When they stepped ashore they anglicized their names. William Fox for instance was born Friedman. Samuel Goldwyn was given the name Goldfish by an immigration officer as the rough equivalent of his unpronounceable Polish name; he was still Goldfish when he formed the Goldwyn company with the Selwyn brothers. After his break with the Selwyns he had to go through the courts to keep his new name: 'A self-made man may prefer a self-made name', said Justice Learned Hand. And Gold-fish remained Goldwyn provided he did not let the name become confused with the company from which he had taken it. An extreme instance of the assertive identity is that of Louis B. Mayer, whose un-anglicized name, like that of the Warners, faded into oblivion. Mayer's Russian documents had all been lost when the time came for the completion of his naturalization papers. The rarely given opportunity to pick an official birthday was therefore presented to him; he chose to have been born, like Yankee Doodle Dandy, on the Fourth of July.

Not that they were ashamed of being Jewish. The older ones married Jewish girls, occasionally attended synagogue during the lifetime of their parents, and were buried after the almost obligatory service in Rabbi Magnin's Hollywood temple. But it was touch and go. There were frequent rumours during his latter years that Mayer was to be received into the Roman Catholic Church by his friend Cardinal Spellman. There were similar reports about the professed atheist Harry Cohn. After his death his Catholic wife had him baptized a Christian. Apparently, *in extremis* in the hospital-bound ambulance Cohn had mentioned the name of Christ though why on this occasion it should have been assumed that the invocation was any less profane than usual is not easy to understand.

Their commitment to the melting pot had many consequences for their work. Possibly it helped them weld together the disparate talents necessary to make a successful team; there were few instances either of racial nepotism or anti-semitism in the industry. Back in 1920, the agent Edward Small approached the newly established Louis B. Mayer with the suggestion that he hire Small's client John Stahl. 'There are no Jewish directors in this business, why don't you give a job to one?' asked Small. The suggestion had cut little ice with William Fox and others, and Mayer only hired Stahl (who turned out to be one of the astutest directors in Hollywood) because he came cheap.

In a brilliant introduction to an anthology of contributions to the Jewish intellectual journal *Commentary*, Alfred Kazin makes some penetrating observations on the role of the Jewish entertainer in America that has considerable bearing on the present discussion :

> But the positive, creative role of the Jew as modern American, and above all as a modern American writer, was in the first year of the century being prepared not in the universities, not even in journalism, but in the vaudeville theatres, music halls, and burlesque houses where the pent-up eagerness of penniless immigrant youngsters met the raw urban scene on its own terms. It was not George Jean Nathan, Robert Nathan, or Ludwig Lewisohn any more than it was Arthur Krock, David Lawrence, Adolph Ochs, or Walter Lippmann, who established the Jew in the national consciousness as a distinctly American figure; it was the Marx Brothers, Eddie Cantor, Al Jolson, Fannie Brice, George Gershwin. Jewish clowns, minstrels, song-writers helped to fit the Jew to America, and America to the Jew, with an élan that made for future creativity in literature as well as the mass products of the 'entertainment industry'.

> . . . in the naturalness and ease with which the Jewish vaudevillian put on blackface, used stereotypes, and ground out popular songs, in the avidity with which the public welcomed him, was the Jew's share in the common experience, the Jew's averageness and typicality, that were to make possible the Jew-as-writer in this country.

> . . . in this country the very poverty and cultural rawness of the Jewish immigrant masses, the self-assertive egalitarianism of the general temper, and the naturalness with which different peoples could identify with each other in the unique halfway house that was New York (without New York it would no doubt all have been different, but without New York there would have been no immigrant epic, no America) gave individual performers the privilege of representing the popular mind.[1]

But the moguls' commitment to the melting pot, to becoming American, also had the effect of making them wish to impose a certain uniformity upon their employees and their product, to advance from a notion that fundamentally everyone is much the same to a demonstration that everyone really *is* the same. Particularly striking is the re-naming of actors and actresses capable of being identified with immigrant groups. So Bernie Swartz

---

[1] *The Commentary Reader*, ed. Norman Podhoretz (London, Rupert Hart-Davis, 1968) pp. xvi-xvii.

became Tony Curtis, Doris Kapplehoff was turned into Doris Day, Carmen Cansino transformed into Rita Hayworth, and so on. As the sociologist E. Digby Baltzell comments[2]: 'Just as the original names of these famous stars suggest the ethnic diversity of talent in America, so their assumed names attest to the Anglo-Saxon ideal which still persists in our culture.'

This process was to backfire on Hollywood in a most unpleasant way during the House Un-American Activities Committee's investigations of the film industry in the late 'forties, a matter I shall be returning to later in more detail. A group of Hollywood artists formed the Committee for the First Amendment to question the HUAC's authority, and its petition was met by this speech to the House of Representatives by the virulently anti-semitic Mississippi congressman, John Rankin, to whom the terms foreigner, Jew and Communist were virtually synonymous:

They sent this petition to Congress and I want to read you some of the names. One of the names is June Havoc. We found that her real name is June Hovick. Another is Danny Kaye, and we found that his real name was David Daniel Kamirsky. Another one here is John Beal, whose real name is J. Alexander Bleidung. Another is Cy Bartlett, whose real name is Sacha Baraniev. Another one is Eddie Cantor, whose real name is Edward Iskowitz. There is one who calls himself Edward Robinson. His real name is Emmanuel Goldenberg. There is another one here who calls himself Melvyn Douglas, whose real name is Melvyn Hesselberg. There are others too numerous to mention. They are attacking the Committee for doing its duty to protect this country and save the American people from the horrible fate the Communists have meted out to the unfortunate Christian people of Europe.

Thus was Rankin able to imply that Hollywood was a nest of spies, all sporting fancy aliases, in the White Anglo-Saxon Protestant camp of America.

Naturally a strong economic interest was involved in this re-

---

[2]*The Protestant Establishment* (London, Secker and Warburg, 1965), p. 47. Though I only quote from it directly this once, Professor Baltzell's illuminating study has greatly influenced the thinking behind my own book.

naming as it was in the provision of entertaining day-dreams. The tycoons reflected the aspirations of the mass public rather than what they truly experienced. This substitution of 'the-way-it-might-be' for 'the-way-it-is' was as much the expression of an ideal as a commercial formula. Even when, after the second world war, anti-semitism became an acceptable subject for movies, it was never suggested that Jews might be in any way different from other members of the community. In *Gentleman's Agreement* (1947) for instance, an honourable and humane film, a gentile poses as a Jew to demonstrate not merely that anti-semitism is a widespread evil but that there is *nothing* that distinguishes Jews from other members of society. During the preparations for the patriotic war movie *Objective Burma* (1945), Jack Warner told the producer during a conference with the screenwriter Alvah Bessie: 'I like the idea of having a Jewish officer in Burma. See that you get a good clean-cut American type for Jacobs.'

As part of this general notion of Americanization, they fought shy of making films that really dealt with Jewish experience. Significantly the two M-G-M film series that most engaged the attention of Louis B. Mayer were those concerning Doctors Kildare and Gillespie, an archetypal story of a surrogate father (or surrogate son), gentiles both; and the Andy Hardy series, idealizing a typical American family. After seeing the rushes of the latest episode of life in Judge Hardy's middletown menage, he would bombard the writers, directors and actors with lengthy memoranda or personally act out whole sequences to show them how it should be done. His furious criticism of mistaken detail (e.g. the way Andy should pray, how he should react to his mother's cooking) had a strongly moral tone. On the question of the quality of the series, however, he had few doubts: 'Don't try to make these films any better. Just keep them the way they are.'

Considering the number of Jewish writers and producers the absence of clearly indentifiable Jewish central characters and settings is quite extraordinary. A rare exception is the first talking (or semi-talking) picture *The Jazz Singer*, a screen version of a schmaltzy stage musical about the reunion of a dying rabbi and his son, a popular crooner. As an image of American religion the film-makers found the extrovert Episcopalian minister or the two-fisted Irish priest more acceptable than the reserved, resigned rabbi. Thus over the years, at important turning points in their histories, the companies have usually turned with great profit to uplifting Christian tales of a generally oecumenical character. In 1927 the silent film version of General Lew Wallace's 'Story of the Christ', *Ben Hur,* helped put M-G-M on the map as an industrial giant just as the 1959 re-make brought M-G-M out of the doldrums. (In the re-make the pagan Romans were played by British actors, and the Jews by Americans, with the very un-semitic Charlton Heston, who earlier had been DeMille's Moses and was later to be George Stevens's John the Baptist, in the title role.) Twentieth Century-Fox chose *The Robe* to launch their CinemaScope process in 1953. It is true that there were also many excursions into the Old Testament, though Cecil B. DeMille's Moses is more reminiscent of George Washington than any Jewish prophet. *The Ten Commandments,* which to use a somewhat inappropriate phrase saved Paramount's bacon in 1956, was advertised in the Far East as a story of a colonial people breaking free from imperialist bondage.

A subject from which Hollywood steered well clear until very recently was Zionism. Consensus movie-making ruled out problems with touchy international implications, and there were the British Commonwealth and Arab markets to consider. The caution proved justified, as it only too often did, when Universal's pro-Israel, mildly anti-British *Sword in the Desert* was withdrawn from a West End cinema in 1949 after public demonstrations. More recent films have handled the subject with kid gloves, balancing out unfavourable British characters with a couple of saintly ones. The most notable picture about the creation of Israel, Otto Preminger's *Exodus,* even managed to be pro-Arab as well as pro-British and finished up placing the real blame on some Nazi intruders.

One of the most indefatigable propagandists and money-raisers for the Zionist cause was the screenwriter Ben Hecht. In 1947 he was denounced in the House of Commons for his outspoken

attacks – often rabidly so – on British policy, and British distributors refused to handle pictures bearing his name. No one came
to his assistance or spoke up on his behalf in Hollywood, and he
was forced to accept much reduced fees for his work and write
under pseudonyms; one name he chose was Robert Emmet,
which sadly enough never got on to a film. In the 'fifties, after the
affair had cooled down, it was the Greek head of Twentieth
Century-Fox, Spyros Skouras, who managed to get the boycott
lifted.

Hecht had been constantly warned by the Hollywood moguls
of the trouble for which he was heading. They were generous
with their contributions to national Jewish charities. (Not always
willingly, though. After being persuaded by Mayer to donate to
the Jewish Relief Fund, Harry Cohn told an aide: 'Relief for
the Jews! Somebody should start a fund for relief *from* the
Jews. All the trouble in the world has been caused by Jews and
Irishmen.') But they drew the line at supporting Zionism. Once
at a Zionist rally Hecht raised pledges of over 100,000 dollars
from an enthusiastic crowd of movie people bowled over by his
oratory, of which he later managed to obtain less than 10,000.
Ultimately he received far more money from the Californian
gambling racketeer Mickey Cohen than from the whole Hollywood community put together.

In the early 'forties Hecht wrote down the names of twenty
Jewish tycoons who might sponsor an appeal for the formation
of a Jewish army in Palestine, to serve as part of the British army
in the second world war. All of them refused point blank, and
Hecht resorted to a trick to win the support of David Selznick.
Echoing the others, Selznick had told him:

I don't want anything to do with your cause for the simple reason
that it's a Jewish political cause. And I am not interested in Jewish
political problems. I'm an American and not a Jew. I'm interested in
this war as an American. It would be silly of me to pretend suddenly
that I'm a Jew, with some sort of full-blown Jewish psychology.

Hecht then challenged Selznick to name three people whom they
should telephone and ask whether they considered him an Amer-

ican or a Jew. If one of them answered 'an American' Selznick would win. None of them did.

Few tycoons could have been described as political animals; the chief exceptions were the prominent Republicans Louis Mayer and Cecil B. DeMille, who was once invited to run for the Senate on the Republican ticket. The majority professed political neutrality. When Harry Cohn put together a documentary about Mussolini in the early 'thirties and remodelled his inner sanctum to resemble Il Duce's office, it was not out of any admiration for fascism but rather because he was taken by the swaggering style of the Italian dictator. The typical attitude to politics was that of Jack Warner who kept two sets of autographed portraits in his office – one of Republican leaders and one of top Democrats. Whenever important political visitors came to the Warner studio, one or other set of photographs would appear on the wall. The industry needed to keep on the right side of the party in power – to obtain preferential legislation, to keep censorship at bay, to acquire military co-operation without which no large-scale war movie could be made. And senior politicians have usually handled the industry with tact and circumspection, being aware of its publicity value. As early as 1896 President McKinley appeared in the first American Biograph show in New York: he was shown campaigning in Ohio, and the short film concluded with the Stars and Stripes filling the screen, an image with which the tycoons were subsequently to regale world audiences unmercifully.

Total neutrality has not always been possible, and whenever Hollywood has had to take political decisions self-interest has invariably triumphed over shaky conviction.

Whatever platitudes about respect for democracy and its institutions they might express themselves or through their films, the tycoons were of a fundamentally reactionary cast when it came to anything that affected them personally. They had come to power in the industry by opposing the Patent Company's monopoly but once entrenched they were not averse to monopolistic practices like keeping foreign films off American screens, block-booking of movies, the preservation of the corporate tie-up between manufacture, distribution and exhibition. They tenaciously exploited their contract performers, lending them out for high fees without increasing their salaries, forcing them into unsuitable roles, and taking them to court or laying them off without salary if they rebelled; but when in the 'fifties they wanted to cut down on contract artists, it was not unknown for the studio heads deliberately to create unpleasant situations to force their stars to leave either without compensation or even by purchasing the remainder of the term. They had grown up in poverty but many of them deeply resented the New Deal when it affected their personal incomes. They had seen or experienced the exploitation of unorganized labour but they firmly opposed unionization within their own industry. The Academy of Motion Picture Arts and Sciences was originally created by Louis Mayer as a company union, and during the 'thirties and 'forties the struggles to create craft guilds were bitter and protracted and impeded at every turn.

One of the consequences of this opposition was the scandalous affairs of the Hollywood branch of IATSE (the International Alliance of Theatrical Stage Employees and Motion Picture Operators of the United States) which covered non-specialist studio workers. During the 'thirties the union fell into the hands of two Chicago racketeers, George E. Browne and Willie Bioff, who blackmailed the corporation heads into paying large sums of money to buy off strikes and wage demands. Their weapon was the threat to close down a studio or call out cinema projectionists across the country. Most of the tycoons were willing to pay up for the sake of industrial peace and also because an honestly run union would have demanded better conditions for its employees. (The major exception was Harry Cohn who refused to pay the levy; as Columbia's president he was the only studio head with power to take the decision and owning few cinemas, was less vulnerable.) This policy, while saving many millions in the short run, was extremely short-sighted and was revealed to the public during an investigation into the muddled financial affairs of Joseph Schenck, chairman of Twentieth Century-Fox and president of the Motion Picture Producers Association. Among other things, in a very complex case, Schenck was unable to account for a certain 100,000 dollars which was clearly earmarked as a pay-off to Willie Bioff. A fall guy for the industry, Schenck was convicted of perjury and sentenced to a year in gaol. As a result of giving evidence that convicted Browne, Bioff and several of their associates, he was released in 1941 after four months inside. He immediately returned to the chairmanship of Fox and in 1947 received a pardon from President Truman and had his forfeited citizenship restored. Schenck had after all always been a staunch supporter of the Democratic Party. Well, not always perhaps. In 1934 he had joined all the other studio heads in throwing Hollywood behind a nonentity called Frank E. Merriam who was running for re-election as Republican governor of California.

Normally the industry did not pay much attention to state elections, as the individual corporations were run from New York and registered in the East. But this was no ordinary election. The Democratic candidate was the socialist writer Upton Sinclair whose local EPIC party took its title from the campaign slogan 'End Poverty in California'. And Sinclair made it clear that the money to realize his utopian dream was to come from the under-taxed rich and the state's burgeoning industry, especially Hollywood. Sinclair had recently published the book *Upton Sinclair Presents William Fox,* a semi-official biography of the deposed tycoon in which he was highly critical of the film business and suggested the possibility of nationalization or at least a measure of federal regulation. Among his most interesting campaign proposals was one made to a New York reporter: 'Why should not the State of California rent one of the idle studios and let the unemployed actors make a few pictures of their own?'

Hollywood was seized by an extraordinary panic. Joe Schenck prophesied that if Sinclair was elected, film production would have to move to Florida, and token negotiations were set afoot to cope with this possibility, though it is hard to believe that anyone could seriously have believed that the industry could have struck its tent so easily or, having done so, that Florida would have been a suitable place to re-pitch it. Studio employees were warned of the consequences of supporting Sinclair and a 'request' went out to everyone earning more than 100 dollars a week to contribute a day's pay to the Merriam cause; this levy, never mentioned in the California press, was first reported in a London newspaper, the now defunct *News Chronicle*. The industry raised a million dollars for the Republican campaign fund.

The most hectic activities went on behind the scenes. Influence was brought to bear on the Democratic Party at national level to persuade Sinclair to withdraw; he refused. This was followed by an elaborate smear campaign – one of the nastiest of the century – involving businessmen throughout the state, the Hearst newspapers, radio stations and the film industry. 'An unbalanced and unscrupulous political speculator,' Hearst called Sinclair. Every cinema in the state showed anti-Sinclair movies of a crudity that revealed only too well the contempt with which the moguls, left to themselves, were capable of viewing their audience. Often these so-called newsreels were clips from old movies, such as a shot from a feature film of young hooligans getting off a train which purported to be a crowd of bums lured to California by the prospect of enjoying the beneficence of Sinclair's welfare state. The most notorious one was a fake newsreel featuring an interview with a menacing figure with a beard and broken accent, a caricature of the Jewish anarchist bogeyman.

'For whom are you voting?' asks the interviewer.
'Vy I am foting for Seenclair.'
'Why are you voting for Mr Sinclair?'
'Vell, his system vorked vell in Russia, vy can't it work here?'

In another newsreel, the inquiring reporter approached a little old lady rocking on her porch.

'For whom are you voting, Mother?'
'I am voting for Governor Merriam.'
'Why, Mother?'
'Because I want to have my little home. It is all I have left in the world.'

The industry's contribution to this campaign has frequently been blamed on Louis B. Mayer, who was vice-chairman of the Republican State Committee. In fact he was out of the country when it got under way. His M-G-M deputy Irving Thalberg, an equally ardent Republican, was one of the master minds. Eleven days before the election, the *Hollywood Reporter* carried the following exultant editorial:

This campaign against Upton Sinclair has been and is dynamite.

When the picture business gets aroused, it becomes AROUSED, and boy, how they can go to it ...

And this activity may reach much further than the ultimate defeat of Mr Sinclair. It will undoubtedly give the big wigs in Washington and politicians all over the country an idea of the real POWER that is in the hands of the industry. Maybe our business will be pampered a bit, instead of being pushed around as it has been since it became a big business.

Before Louis B. Mayer, Irving Thalberg, Charles Pettijohn (a good old democrat under ordinary conditions) [legal counsel to the Hays Office] and Carey Wilson [M-G-M writer and producer of the Andy Hardy and Dr Gillespie series] stepped in this political battle here, the whole Republican party seemed to have been sunk by the insane promises of Mr Sinclair. With that group in the war, and it has been a WAR, things took a very different turn. Governor Merriam's party here in the South had a HEAD, something that was missing before. It received the finances it so direly needed AND the whole picture business got behind the shove.

Sinclair is not defeated yet, but indications point to it, and California should stand up and sing hosannas for their greatest State industry, MOTION PICTURES, and the same industry should, for itself, point to its work whenever some of the screwy legislation comes up in the various State legislatures during the next few months.

In the election Sinclair was soundly thrashed, and if the part that the film industry had taken in achieving this result may have been exaggerated, it was one of which its leaders had every reason to feel deeply ashamed.[3] The upshot was the creation of

[3]A good deal of credit for Sinclair's defeat belongs to Campaigns, Inc., a Californian public relations organization founded by the San Francisco husband-and-wife team, Clem Whitaker and Leone Baxter, pioneers in the field of political PR. Their elaborate smear job was the firm's first big outing and they went on to handle such projects as the American Medical Association's multi-million dollar campaign against 'socialized medicine'. In his study of American PR firms *The Image Merchants* (London, Weidenfeld and Nicolson, 1960), Irwin Ross reports Leone Baxter as looking back over a quarter of a century to the Sinclair affair and reflecting thus: 'We wouldn't operate like that now, would we, Clem?'.

an interest in politics among Hollywood artists that had not previously existed. Screen-writers were not to forget for a long time
the contemptuous words of Louis B. Mayer spoken to a gathering of his staff: 'What does Sinclair know about anything? He's
just a writer.'

The upsurge of political activity that followed the Merriam-
Sinclair contest was to have its tragic consequences in the years
after the second world war. For it led many people into lending
their support to organizations that the more politically sophisti-
cated might have recognized as Communist-inspired. However,
during the late 'thirties and early 'forties Communists worked
fairly openly in Hollywood, even if they did not always brandish
their party membership cards openly in their employers' faces.
Their influence was strong in the Screenwriters Guild, in left-
wing fund-raising groups, and sometimes, never especially effec-
tively, they attempted to impose their will on the industry. They
prevented Mussolini's son and the Nazi film director Leni
Riefenstahl from working in California, for example, and there
are instances of attempts to keep pro-German themes out of
films; but you did not need to be a Communist to support these
moves. Communists almost certainly helped each other get jobs
and contributed a good deal to party funds, though generally less
than such well-heeled comrades might be expected to have done.
But their general behaviour, their worship of money and success,
differed little from that of apolitical Hollywood contemporaries.
Bertolt Brecht was denied a major credit on his single American
movie when a credit-hungry Communist scriptwriter, who
initially had been brought in mainly as a translator, took over the
script and totally distorted Brecht's work;[4] and Budd Schulberg

[4]There are conflicting accounts of Brecht's script for *Hangmen Also Die*
(1942), a war movie about the assassination of Heydrich by the Czech under-
ground. Brecht told the House Un-American Activities Committee: 'I sold a
story to Hollywood but I did not write the screenplay myself'. According to
Martin Esslin (in *Brecht, A Choice of Evils*, 1959, p. 64) 'the final product
bore little resemblance to Brecht's outline and he dissociated himself from it';
another biographer John Willett (*The Theatre of Bertolt Brecht*, 1959, p. 65)
concurs: 'Brecht thought that his contribution had been distorted and brought
a case to ensure the credits distinguished it from the actual script.' Fritz
Lang, however, who directed the movie and suggested the original idea to

quit the Party after Communist pressure had been brought to bear on him not to publish *What Makes Sammy Run?*, the grounds being that the novel was too critical of the industry.

There was however no Communist influence to speak of on what actually went on in the movies. No amount of probing by right-wing critics or subsequent self-justification by Communist and ex-Communist writers has been able to challenge this verdict. When Lillian Hellman saw a film with a Spanish Civil War setting written by Hollywood's leading Communist author John Howard Lawson, she was scarcely able to distinguish between the two sides.

'The Communists hate and fear the American motion picture. It is their number one hate,' said Eric Johnston, the post-war president of the MPPA, with some measure of exaggeration, although he might well have believed that it was true. His predecessor, Will Hays, was always pleased to point out the universality of Hollywood's appeal by citing Hitler's unwavering enthusiasm for American pictures which, when seized during the war, were hastened to the Fuehrer's private cinema.

In 1940 the House of Representatives Committee on Un-American Activities (HUAC) in the third year of its noisy, noisome existence, took a look at Hollywood to question its premature anti-fascism, and withdrew after making little impact. The situation was different when the Committee started its investigation of Communist infiltration of Hollywood in 1947. Such a series of hearings had been important to the Committee's first chairman, Martin Dies of Texas, and his chief lieutenant, John Rankin, both Democrats, but violently anti-British, anti-Hollywood, and anti-semitic, and to the present chairman, J.

his friend Brecht, tells us that the scenarist John Wexley 'wanted to have a sole credit for the screenplay' and 'got it despite the fact that Hanns Eisler, the composer, and I both went in front of the Screen Writers Guild and swore that many, many scenes were written by Brecht and that nobody else, certainly not Mr Wexley, could have done them. But they said, "Well, Mr Brecht will go back to Germany but Mr Wexley will stay here. Mr Wexley will need the credit much more than Mr Brecht".' (*Fritz Lang in America* by Peter Bogdanovich, p. 60). Brecht was the first victim of the House Un-American Activities Committee's post-war enquiry and went back to Germany; Wexley was a later Committee victim and found himself on Hollywood's black-list.

Parnell Thomas, a Republican from New Jersey, who saw great opportunities for grabbing the headlines and discrediting the New Deal. Initially the industry stood firm.

There was no shortage of friendly witnesses to testify to the presence of Communists in Hollywood, and indeed there was reason to believe that the ultra-right wing Motion Picture Alliance for the Preservation of American Ideals had played some part in arranging the inquiry. Louis B. Mayer and Jack Warner spoke at length, sometimes incoherently, sometimes in a pathetically grovelling manner that ill became men wielding such power. Both were at pains to excuse the pro-Russian pictures that had been produced at their studios during the war. No one who spoke seemed much afraid of working with left-wing writers, not even members of the Motion Picture Alliance. The suave character actor Adolphe Menjou, one of the Alliance's stalwarts and a self-styled expert on communism, told the Committee: 'We have many Communists who are splendid writers. They do not have to write communistically at all, but they have to be watched.' And Jack Warner informed the inquisitors that no political propaganda ever escaped his eagle eye, despite some cunning attempts, and added: 'I can't for the life of me figure where men could get together to deprive a man of his livelihood because of his political beliefs.' Much of the testimony, from such as Ginger Rogers's mother and Gary Cooper, was confused and unpersuasive. 'From what I hear I don't like it because it isn't on the level,' said Cooper of communism.

The inquiry, however, came to centre on the refusal to answer questions concerning their political beliefs by ten 'unfriendly' witnesses – two directors, seven writers, and one producer – who stood on their constitutional rights under the First Amendment and were cited for contempt of Congress. All were, or had been, Communists, but that was not really the issue when the investigation began, not to Hollywood at least; the issues were on the one hand whether Communists influenced film-making, and on the other the right of individual citizens in peacetime to keep their personal political allegiance to themselves. The ten were the screenwrtiers John Howard Lawson, Alvah Bessie,

Dalton Trumbo, Lester Cole, Albert Maltz, Samuel Ornitz, Ring Lardner Jr; the producer-writer-director Herbert Biberman; the writer-producer Adrian Scott; and the director Edward Dmytryk. None of them was a major Hollywood figure but unfair attempts have been made to pour scorn on their work by the simple method of listing the trivial-sounding movies to which they had contributed; actually between them they had, by prevailing industrial standards, some impressive credits. Two or three of them might be written off as nonentities; the rest were respected artists of some standing, though as was the case with most writers and directors, little known to the general public. Sadly, the conduct of most of 'the Hollywood Ten' or 'the Unfriendly Ten', as they came to be called, appeared devious and undignified, even if the latter posture was forced on them by the confused manner in which HUAC conducted its affairs; and they tended to meet the hectoring Committee with the same kind of patriotic jargon with which they were themselves confronted. For a couple of the group, this was their finest hour as they attempted to say to the Committee some of the things they had never been able to get into their pictures. It has even been suggested that some might have had a masochistic desire to be punished for their years of high living (the isolated, sybaritic life of Hollywood and the guilt it induced has often been cited as a factor contributing to the relatively high membership of the Communist Party there; another frequently mentioned factor was the movie colony's predilection for extreme gestures and histrionic behaviour). John Howard Lawson had once written of his work in a Communist journal that 'I do not hesitate to say that it is my aim to present the Communist position and to do so in the most specific manner'; now he shouted at the Committee: 'I am not on trial here, Mr Thomas. This Committee is on trial before the American people. Let us get that straight.'

If the Ten believed, as at first they were led to believe both by the statements of their employers and the actions of their fellow artists, that the industry would stand behind them, they were soon doomed to disappointment. Had the moguls stood fast at this time it is just possible that the whole post-war history of loyalty investigations might have been changed and the influence of the Committee and similar bodies nipped in the bud. But they did not, and while one cannot see the HUAC Hollywood investigation apart from the overall American post-war scene, the reason for the tycoons' sudden capitulation at that precise moment was pressure from the bankers. As Ed Sullivan wrote in his New York *Daily News* column:

> Reason that Hollywood big shots rushed to New York and barred the 10 cited by Congress was forecast in my Nov. 1st column: 'Hollywood has been dealt a body blow that won't please Wall Street financiers, who have not less than 600,000,000 dollars in picture companies.' Wall Street juggled the strings, that's all.

Sullivan was referring to the meeting of representatives of the Motion Picture Assocation of America, the Association of Motion Picture Producers and the Society of Independent Motion Picture Producers which was held at the Waldorf-Astoria Hotel and produced the so-called Waldorf Declaration. The Declaration was opposed by Samuel Goldwyn, who had never had any personal obligation to the bankers, and by the liberal Dore Schary, then head of production at RKO. But they were in no position to press their disagreement. The deadly declaration read thus:

> Members of the Association of Motion Picture Producers deplore the action of the ten Hollywood men who have been cited for contempt of the House of Representatives. We do not desire to pre-judge their legal rights, but their actions have been a disservice to their employers and have impaired their usefulness to the industry.
>
> We will forthwith discharge or suspend without compensation those in our employ and we will not re-employ any of the ten until such time as he is acquitted or has purged himself of contempt and declares himself under oath that he is not a Communist.
>
> On the broader issue of alleged subversion and disloyal elements in Hollywood, our members are likewise prepared to take positive action. We will not knowingly employ a Communist or a member of any party or group which advocates the overthrow of the United States by force or by any illegal or unconstitutional methods.
>
> In pursuing this policy, we are not going to be swayed by hysteria

or intimidation from any source. We are frank to recognise that such a policy involves dangers and risks. There is the danger of hurting innocent people. There is the risk of creating an atmosphere of fear. Creative work at its best cannot be carried on in an atmosphere of fear. We will guard against this danger, this risk, this fear.

To this end we will invite the Hollywood talent guilds to work with us to eliminate any subversives; to protect the innocent; and to safeguard free speech and a free screen wherever threatened.

The absence of a national policy, established by Congress with respect to the employment of Communists in private industry, makes our task difficult. Ours is a nation of laws. We request Congress to enact legislation to assist American industry to rid itself of subversive, disloyal elements.

Nothing subversive or un-American has appeared on the screen. Nor can any number of Hollywood investigations obscure the patriotic services of the 30,000 Americans employed in Hollywood who have given our government invaluable aid in war and peace.

The document was signed by all the heads of studios and by Eric Johnston who happened to be president of both the MPAA and the AMPP. Breathtaking in its constant contradictions, shocking in its cravenness, yielding far more to the industry's opponents than they had ever dared to ask, the Waldorf Declaration was the pathetic product of insecure, worried and self-evidently unprincipled men. From that point on the moguls lost control of the situation. They had by their solemn Declaration turned the chaotic farce of the HUAC hearings into a grim industrial tragedy. The Declaration was a positive invitation not only to the HUAC to come again but to every publicity-seeking, Red-hunting busybody to enter the portals. However, a matter of weeks after the Declaration, Eric Johnston had the gall to go before a public service gathering in Philadelphia to pick up an award made to the film *Crossfire,* a thriller attacking anti-semitism, produced by the suspended producer Adrian Scott and directed by another of the Unfriendly Ten, Edward Dmytryk. Dore Schary, under whose liberal aegis at RKO the picture had been made, had the good taste not to attend.

An unofficial black-list grew up to which many other names were added when, in 1951, against the background of McCarthy-ism and the Korean War, the House Committee resumed its hearings on Hollywood and other studio employees refused to testify about their political pasts and thus be involved in naming former associates, or did so and came out with a string of names. In the second wave of hearings there was the difference that the moguls themselves were not under pressure, and no further mention was made about the Communist influence on any particular films. All the Committee wanted was names and more names – though it was merely a ritual process, for they had the names of former Communists and left-wingers already. The black list was further swelled by the contribution of names from rosters of suspects compiled on the slimmest evidence by right-wing patriotic groups like the American Legion; as the lists were never made public, no one could ever know for certain whether by some mischance, malice or false suspicion his name might be on one. The job of reinstating black-listed artists fell to outsiders, most prominently the one-time Nebraska movie-house projectionist Roy Brewer, International Representative of IATSE, the theatrical stage employees' union. Brewer, a tough, right-wing survivor of the 'forties union conflicts, became the number one clearance expert, and he demanded repentance and the naming of names to secure rehabilitation. Apart from running IATSE, Brewer was on the executive committees of both the Motion Picture Alliance for the Preservation of American Ideals and the Motion Picture Industry Council, a solidarity group formed in 1949 to represent the joint interests of the twelve principal organizations to which producers, artists and craftsmen belonged. Speaking on behalf of Hollywood, the Industry Council issued this statement at the height of the Korean War:

This country is engaged in a war with Communism. Eighty-seven thousand American casualties leave little room for witnesses to stand on the First and Fifth Amendments; and for those who do we have no sympathy. In time of crisis, we believe that the demands of American patriotism make necessary that witnesses respond to the call of their country, as represented by your Committee, and give you all the information necessary to the success of your objective.

Hollywood was running scared over whom it employed and the

kind of pictures it made. 'This is a time for expediency, not integrity,' one producer told an actress who was threatened with the possibility of being black-listed unless she publicly disavowed not her Communist sympathies (she had never had any) but her former criticism of the House Committee's smear techniques.

The Unfriendly Ten unsuccessfully appealed against their gaol sentences for contempt of Congress and then served their sentences; eight did a year inside, two were committed for six months, all paid a thousand dollar fine. One of them had the ironic privilege of being confined in the same federal penitentiary as Parnell Thomas, the former HUAC chairman, who had been convicted of embezzling government funds. No one else in Hollywood went to gaol, because subsequent witnesses sought the protection of the Fifth Amendment (against self-incrimination) which did not involve them in contempt proceedings. The only other person seriously threatened with gaol was the top screenwriter Sidney Buchman who testified without taking the Fifth that he had been a member of the Communist Party from 1938 to 1945, but refused, on principle, to name fellow Party members; through a legal technicality (there had initially been no Committee quorum and a subsequent hearing was postponed owing to his ill-health), he escaped with a mere 150 dollar fine and a year's suspended sentence. Throughout the time of his party membership, Buchman had been a top Columbia screenwriter and personal friend of Harry Cohn. Columbia's president was apparently very sorry to see him go, and Buchman was indeed the only victim of the Hollywood witch-hunts who was at all closely associated with any of the moguls. (He returned to movies much later and in 1966 adapted and produced the excellent film version of Mary McCarthy's *The Group*.)

Hundreds of talented men like Buchman were driven out of the industry. Many later went through the ritual of clearance and returned shriven to the fold; Edward Dmytryk, who had stood by his fellow members of the Ten mainly through loyalty, made his public confession shortly after he was released from gaol, for he had actually quit the Party, as had his friend Adrian Scott, before the 1947 hearings. Many went into other jobs. A number left to work in Europe. Not a few writers continued to work for low sums under pseudonyms or by using other authors as fronts, and several Oscars went to these bootleg scripts. In England, for instance, the black-listed director Joseph Losey and the black-listed writer Carl Foreman made *The Sleeping Tiger* (1954) together, using respectively the names Victor Hanbury and Derek Frye; not until 1957, even in England was Losey able to sign his own work. For actors with recognizable faces and voices there was little chance of employment either in films or in broadcasting. When some black-listed artists got together and made an independent left-wing movie called *Salt of the Earth* (directed by the Ten's Herbert Biberman), they found it impossible to get their admittedly rather poor picture shown publicly in American cinemas.

So Hollywood continued on its jittery way with this further traumatic shock to add to the steady undermining of confidence that the competition from television had brought, and the divorce of production and exhibition, and the competition from foreign and overseas-located movies were bringing. The studios attempted to win public favour with strongly anti-Communist movies, mostly made between 1948 and 1953. When these proved unsuccessful at the box-office they were soon abandoned. Gradually, however, the black-listed artists began to re-emerge under their own names, after a period in which the real authorship of various pseudonymous screenplays had been public knowledge: Academy Awards in three consecutive years went to such scripts. The first people to employ them openly were independent producers, like Otto Preminger, who gave Dalton Trumbo, the most talented author among the Ten, his first real credit for thirteen years as screenwriter on *Exodus* in 1960. But even today the Hollywood witch-hunt casts its long shadow in the unhealed wounds of broken lives and ruptured friendships, disrupted careers and lingering suspicions. Despite the fact that Trumbo emerged from pseudonymity in 1960 with his name on *Exodus* and *Spartacus* the Ten remained industrial dynamite as Frank Sinatra, supposedly the most influential star in Hollywood, found to his cost when he announced that year that he had hired

Albert Maltz to write a screenplay from William Bradford Huie's book *The Execution of Private Slovik*, a controversial study of the pathetic GI in the second world war who had the unfortunate fate of being the only American army deserter to be shot since the Civil War. Sinatra was lashed by editorials in the Hearst press and publicly denounced by John Wayne and the late Ward Bond, both leading members of Hollywood's right wing. Sinatra took a full-page ad in the trade press to announce that

I am prepared to stand on my principles and to await the verdict of the American people when they see *The Execution of Private Slovik*. I repeat: In my role as a picture-maker, I have – in my opinion – hired the best man for the job.

Less than three weeks after his first announcement, Sinatra backed down. 'Due to the reactions of my family, my friends and the American public,' he said, 'I have instructed my attorneys to make a settlement with Albert Maltz and to inform him that he will not write the screenplay for *The Execution of Private Slovik*.' And the picture was never made. A rumour circulated at the time that the principal influence on Sinatra came from Joseph Kennedy who is said to have instructed the crooner that either he got rid of Maltz or else totally dissociated himself from John F. Kennedy's presidential campaign which the decision to employ Maltz was liable to hurt. There were also other dangers: during the brief period in which Sinatra stood by Maltz, several of his friends lost television sponsors. Even if he had persisted with the projected movie, the singer has since said, it is unlikely that the banks would have provided the necessary money.

Perhaps Sinatra found some little compensatory satisfaction three years later when his recording of 'Have Yourself a Merry Little Christmas' was used as an ironic soundtrack accompaniment to the military execution of an American soldier in Europe during the second world war in *The Victors*, the first directorial assignment of the formerly black-listed Hollywood writer Carl Foreman.

One can see in the situation brought about by the HUAC inquiry the genuine confusion in the minds of the tycoons. Such indefinable terms as All-American, Un-American, one hundred per cent American, were part of their personal rhetoric, which reflected their vague ideal of assimilation and very often determined the tone of their movies. They had never clearly thought out their positions or understood their power. They had mortgaged their authority to the bankers and been incapable of redeeming it. Now they were the victims of their own insecurity, unable to stand up either for their employees or for themselves. Their belief that 'the public is always right' had also exploded in their face once more.

The days of the great studios were over by the time Hollywood had recovered from this blow. To their credit many moguls deeply regretted what had happened. One who did not was the arch-political intriguer Louis B. Mayer. After a lifetime devoted to the service of the Republican Party the ageing Mayer swung further and further to the right. He fell out with his son-in-law, the producer William Goetz, largely over politics, and never spoke to him again after Goetz had allowed his home to be used to hold a Hollywood reception for Adlai Stevenson during the 1952 election campaign. In 1954 Mayer made a sentimental journey to Haverhill, Massachussetts, the town in which nearly fifty years before he had opened his first cinema. And there the embittered ex-boss of M-G-M reaffirmed his belief in America. 'The more McCarthy yells, the better I like him,' said Mayer. 'He's doing a job to get rid of the termites eating away at our democracy. I don't care how many toes he steps on, including mine, as long as he gets the job done. I hope he drives all the bums back to Moscow. That's the place for them.' Mayer was, of course, born in Minsk.

9

THE CRUMBLING PYRAMID

Is it, perhaps, a blessing of the Divine
Projectionist that the reels nearest 'The End'
move more swiftly? Is he gently reminding us
that the work we have left must be our best work,
for there is no time for anything less than our
best?

Cecil B. DeMille

When Chaplin, Fairbanks, Griffith and Pickford formed United Artists fifty years ago one of their erstwhile employers quipped that 'the lunatics have taken over the asylum'. The company was never a major success until the early 1950s when, under new management and unburdened by costly studios, it was remodelled to cater for the independent companies which were rapidly coming to dominate the industry. The six remaining major studios now exist largely to provide the fifty-odd influential independent producers with sound stages, distribution facilities, and often, but not always, financial backing. Gone are the rosters of contract artists and, with fewer cinemas and only a handful of them owned by the companies, there is no need to produce feature movies on an assembly-line basis. The assembly line has been rejigged for the manufacture of television programmes to which Hollywood is primarily devoted, and which keep its technicians profitably employed. Television of course insists upon a steady production of feature films too, for the small screen has found nothing that attracts audiences as consistently as old movies.

Agents now superintend the fortunes of most stars and any large-scale picture is the result of temporary alliances between a number of companies. As Richard Zanuck, currently occupying his father's former place as production head at Twentieth Century-Fox, says:

Now at most we have arrangements with a star or a director that he will make one or two films with us, but even then the negotiations

128

required to bring together a property, a writer, a director and two or three suitable stars, all of whom are their own masters with probably their own companies, becomes a major exercise.

The system has its advantages. No longer does one studio boss attempt to put his hand or stamp his tastes on everything that happens on his lot. More personal, adventurous movie-making can result – and sometimes does. But with more money invested in the average single picture than before, there is as much chance that an independent producer will interfere (or a star, if he has a major say in the production) as would an old-style studio chief. Still, a director or writer nowadays has a greater opportunity to be his own producer or to dictate his personal terms. Yet some have looked back nostalgically to the old days, forgetting perhaps what they once endured. 'We made pictures then, we didn't make deals,' says Billy Wilder. 'Today we spend eighty per cent of our time making deals and twenty per cent making pictures.' It can also be argued that changes in public taste, less rigid censorship, the competition of television, and the fact that successful formulae seem harder than ever to come by, have played a greater part in improving movies than the passing of the studios – that is of course if one accepts that the improvement has been all that marked.

Not only are the big studios a shadow of their former selves but the founding moguls' successors are for the most part a colourless crowd, businessmen little committed to the cinema. And they preside over diversified empires concerned with pharmaceuticals, hotels, food products, oil, underwear, real estate, in which movies play only a part and not necessarily the most profitable one. The moguls' true heirs are the independent producers, among whom a few of the old-timers live on: Hal Wallis, for example, still running his independent unit at Paramount. Nevertheless, Hollywood has remained a place where the accent is upon youth, whether real or simulated, and has become increasingly aware of the need to court young audiences and encourage youthful talent. Richard Zanuck, for instance, was under thirty when he took charge of the Twentieth Century-Fox lot, while Robert Evans, the former child radio actor, movie star (e.g. *The Sun Also Rises, The Fiend that Walks the West*) and independent producer, was a mere thirty-six when in 1966 he became vice-president in charge of production at Paramount.

With a few exceptions, like Wallis, Jack Warner and Darryl Zanuck, most of the major figures from Hollywood's years of greatness are now dead or in reluctant retirement. They usually died in office or were thrust out against their will. Once outside they fought to return; like Louis B. Mayer who was plotting against the M-G-M régime up to his dying day, or Ben Schulberg who placed ads in the trade press vainly pleading for work. Only a few accepted retirement gracefully; Joe Brandt was one of them – he left Columbia while still in his early forties to get away from the feuding Cohn brothers and enjoy his wealth in international travel, but he was dead before reaching his fiftieth birthday. Carl Laemmle spent the last three, unemployed years of his life entertaining friends to dinner and making jokes about his large collection of ill-fitting dentures – 'just listen to these teeth rattle'. Many of them must have felt like Harry Cohn when he dismissed the idea of giving up the presidency of Columbia:

No, I won't do it. Sitting behind this desk, I can always press a buzzer and get somebody to talk to me. If I wasn't head of a studio, who would talk to me? Who would come to my house for dinner? No, I won't do it.

They had not, however, been great planners for the future. They left the preservation of the films they produced to others once the commercial value had gone from them; they invested a shamelessly small amount in technical research, from the lack of which the industry is still suffering; they were almost invariably lacking in foresight at the most crucial junctures – both the coming of sound and the advent of television, for instance, found them acting slowly and indecisively. They were living in a world they knew could not long endure. Nevertheless, at least for the moment, seven of the eight major organizations still carry on under their new managements, even if Warner Brothers is now Warner Brothers-Seven Arts, having been swallowed up by a prosperous independent company whose films it once distributed, and M-G-M have on their posters a new, more modish, less ferocious lion. But the old studio styles – formed from a combination of cast, subject, treatment, technical standards and so on, that reflected some corporately shaped taste – have largely disappeared. Each studio's movies had a particular look, even their black and white photography looked different, due to the standards established in their laboratories and by their resident designers. M-G M, for instance, was always the 'class' studio, with tastefully mounted, glossy musicals, high life melodrama and society comedies; its stars were generally ladies and gentlemen of a certain culture and poise like Clark Gable and Greer Garson, whom Louis B. Mayer brought over from Britain and made into the queen mother of the M-G-M lot. Reflecting the twin drives of Mayer, M-G-M alternated between the unrealistically classy and the idealistically folksy – for it was also the studio of the Andy Hardy series whose juvenile lead, Mickey Rooney, was three years running (1939-41) named Hollywood's top money-making star. (Of course when Dore Schary came to M-G-M from RKO he brought with him his predilection for 'message' films.) Warner Brothers on the other hand was always more down to earth with its reputation for crime movies, 'social conscience' pictures, historical biographies and sharp melodrama; the Warner Brothers men were short, tough, aggressive, like Edward G. Robinson, Humphrey Bogart and Jimmy Cagney, its women, with Bette Davis pre-eminent, were more waspish, less lady-like than M-G-M's. When Warners turned to musicals they rarely dealt in fantasy, preferring instead musical biographies. As many other moviegoers did, I knew instinctively as a child, without knowing anything about the companies or indeed about how films were made, more or less what I was in for – what a film would look like, feel like – as soon as I had seen the studio trademark appear at the beginning. When Martha asks George in *Who's Afraid of Virginia Woolf?* to help recall 'some goddamn Warner Brothers' epic' she is touching on this particular feeling for studio style as well as revealing her age; though eventually released by Warner Brothers, the film version of Edward Albee's play did not look particularly like any Warner Brothers' epic, as it might have done twenty years before with Bette Davis and Paul Henreid as Martha and George, and directed by Michael Curtiz from a script carefully tailored to the requirements of the Hays Office. The movies were not, except on rare occasions, about current reality but about current tastes, or the way that the moguls and their employees interpreted them. A certain kind of reality is there, a reality refracted but nevertheless even at a distance of many years capable of being decoded by the social historian or the casual viewer. Irving Thalberg has certainly been proved correct in the modest claim he made in a 1929 address at the University of Southern California: 'I believe that although the motion picture will not live forever as a work of art, except in a few instances, it will be the most effective way of showing posterity how we live now.'

The names of the moguls continue to be seen on the credits of the old films they produced. Some live on in the titles of their former companies – Fox, the Warners, Goldwyn and Mayer; others are remembered in street names around Beverly Hills, in footprints left in the forecourt of Grauman's Chinese Theatre, on the red and gold stars let into the sidewalk along Hollywood Boulevard, through plaques at studio entrances and titles of company buildings, and in the names of favourite dishes still served in the canteens. While many were followed into the business by their sons, very few of the latter succeeded either in matching their fathers' achievements or even in carrying on the business themselves. Perhaps only David Selznick can be said to have significantly surpassed his father.

I once asked a celebrated writer who had worked under most of the moguls which he thought deserved the title of 'the worst tycoon'. 'I guess you'd need a pair of jeweller's scales,' he said, 'to make such a fine calculation.' This is, I fancy, a somewhat uncharitable opinion, but towards the end the tycoons themselves were taking a rather jaundiced view of their creation. 'You see, it's not a business. It's a racket!' Harry Cohn said to the reporter Ezra Goodman in one of his last interviews; and walking through Hollywood one day in the 'fifties a gloomy David Selznick told Ben Hecht: 'Hollywood's like Egypt. Full of crumbled pyramids.

It'll never come back. It'll just keep on crumbling until finally the wind blows the last studio props across the sand.' Pyramids do not disintegrate quite so easily. When a proposal came up recently to abolish the suburb of Hollywood and absorb it into Los Angeles, one of the successful opponents of the scheme made a counter-proposal. It would be better, he suggested, to change the name of Los Angeles to Hollywood.

Looking back to those days, now nearly sixty years ago, when the four thousand citizens of the unknown Hollywood were forced, by the very aridity of their zone, to join Los Angeles, we might well agree with Sam Goldwyn who said (in a genuine Goldwynism recorded during a reminiscent discussion with Ezra Goodman), 'We have all passed a lot of water since then.'

BIOGRAPHICAL NOTES

PANDRO S. BERMAN (1905–)

Pittsburgh-born son of movie pioneer Harry Berman, who was general manager at Universal and later at the Film Booking Office of America, the company through which Joseph Kennedy entered the industry. Pandro began as an assistant director and editor at FBO, then served as film and title editor at Columbia before returning to FBO's successor RKO, where he became chief editor and subsequently assistant to the vice-president in charge of production, William Le Baron (a playwright and magazine editor, who at various times worked for Hearst's Cosmopolitan Films, Paramount, Twentieth Century-Fox, and his own Federal Films), and Le Baron's successor, David Selznick. During the 'thirties he was a producer at RKO. In 1940 Berman joined M-G-M where he produced a wide variety of successful big-budget films for over twenty years, eventually turning to independent production. Unquestionably the later M-G-M style was determined by his pictures and those of his colleague Arthur Freed (who joined M-G-M the same year and specialized in musicals) in the way that earlier M-G-M movies were influenced by the tastes of Irving Thalberg. To the general public he is best known on account of the enthusiasm shown for his work by Gore Vidal's Myra Breckinridge. Of his departure from M-G-M, Myra observed: 'How tragic! M-G-M without Pandro S. Berman is like the American flag without its stars.'

HARRY COHN (1891-1958)

Born on the New York East Side, third son of orthodox Jewish parents, father a German immigrant tailor, mother from Poland.

Worked as trolley-bus conductor, vaudeville performer (with composer Harry Ruby) and song plugger. Entered films in 1918 as secretary to Carl Laemmle for whom elder brother Jack (1889-1956) and Jack's friend Joe Brandt worked. Formed CBS Sales Company in 1920 with Brandt and brother Jack, which became Columbia Pictures in 1924. His first wife's sizeable divorce settlement enabled the company to expand. In 1932, with the assistance of banker A. P. Giannini, Cohn resisted Jack's attempt to overthrow him, and on Brandt's retirement that year Cohn became Columbia president as well as remaining head of production in Hollywood. He hung on to both positions until his death. Said to be the inspiration for the junk merchant Harry Brock in Garson Kanin's stage comedy *Born Yesterday* (1946) and for the movie tycoon Marcus Hoff in Clifford Odet's play *The Big Knife* (1952), as well as for Broderick Crawford's Academy Award-winning portrayal of Willie Stark in the 1949 film version of Robert Penn Warren's novel *All the King's Men*. The fact should not be overlooked that both *Born Yesterday* and *All the King's Men* were Columbia movies, and that Clifford Odets wrote the eulogy, spoken by Danny Kaye, for Harry Cohn's funeral. He is the subject of a well-researched and highly entertaining biography, *King Cohn,* by Bob Thomas (New York, Putnam, 1967; London, Barrie and Rockliff, 1967).

CECIL B. DEMILLE (1881-1959)

Descendant of a long-established southern family of Anglo-Dutch extraction and born in Ashfield, Mass. Father studied to be an Episcopalian minister but was never ordained and became a teacher and playwright. Cecil's elder brother was playwright and director William C. deMille (father of choreographer Agnes). Acted with touring companies until 1913 when, unemployed and considering taking part in the Mexican revolution, he joined Jesse Lasky and Sam Goldwyn in forming Lasky Feature Plays; directed their first film *The Squaw Man* in Hollywood. Started his own company in 1923 with DeMille studios; then briefly with M-G-M in the late 'twenties, before returning to head a production unit at Paramount where he worked until his death, directing epic adventure and biblical movies, the last being *The Ten Commandments* (1956). With the coming of sound it had appeared that his days were numbered, but DeMille soon recovered and remained Hollywood's greatest primitive artist until the end, when he was preparing an 'epic' history of the Scouting movement, *Be Prepared*. He also worked extensively in radio until 1944 when he refused to pay the dollar-a-member levy sought by the American Federation of Radio Artists to fight a Californian ballot proposal to abolish closed shops. His refusal forced him out of radio (on which he made a hundred thousand dollars a year) and as a result he set up the DeMille Foundation for Political Freedom to campaign for anti-closed shop 'right to work' laws. The Foundation was dissolved after his death. *The Autobiography of Cecil B. DeMille* edited by Donald Hayne was published posthumously (New York, Prentice-Hall, 1959; London, W. H. Allen, 1960). His brother William has written a sharper, more amusing and critical autobiography, *Hollywood Saga* (New York, Dutton, 1939).

WALT DISNEY (1901-66)

Born in Chicago; studied art and photography in high school, and became commercial artist after Red Cross service in the first world war: drawing cinema slides for an advertising firm in Kansas City. Went to Hollywood in 1923 with elder brother Roy (who managed the business side and later became president of Walt Disney Productions). Made films combining cartoons and live actors, later marrying an actress who appeared in them. After many minor successes he achieved first major impact with third Mickey Mouse cartoon, shown with sound accompaniment in 1928, and with first colour cartoon in 1932. Released pictures through Columbia, United Artists and RKO until he set up his own distribution system. During the 1930s he built up a large organization of artists whose work he superintended. In 1938 he made his first feature-length cartoon, *Snow White and the Seven Dwarfs*. After the second world war he branched out into nature documentaries and non-cartoon feature films directed at juvenile audiences, and in the early 'fifties moved into television. In 1955 he opened the Disneyland amusement park at Anaheim, Los Angeles.

The best book on Disney was the semi-official *The Art of Walt Disney* by Robert Feild (New York, Macmillan, 1942; London, Collins, 1944), until the recent, admirable and totally unauthorized *The Disney Version* by Richard Schickel (New York, Simon and Schuster, 1968), published in Britain as *Walt Disney*, (Weidenfeld & Nicolson, 1968).

WILLIAM FOX (1879-1952)

Born in Tulchva, Hungary; came to the United States when he was nine months old, with Jewish parents of German descent. Left school at eleven to join his father in the garment industry. Was married at twenty-one to a local girl and set up his own shrinking and examining business. Entered films in Brooklyn with a penny arcade which developed into a chain of fifteen cinemas, and then started his film exchange, The Greater New York Rental Company, which the Patent Company unsuccessfully attempted to acquire. Moved into production in 1912 with a company that became the Fox Film Corporation (1915). He first made minor movies (for which his wife supplied stories culled from women's magazines). During the 'twenties he conducted the first experiments with sound-on-film, and also investigated the possibilities of the wide screen. In 1929 he acquired the Gaumont chain in Britain and attempted to take over Loew's Inc. The failure of this bid, due to the Wall Street crash, Justice Department intervention, and his own temporary disablement after a car crash, led to his being pushed out of his own company. In 1936 he filed a bankruptcy petition and in 1942 went to gaol for a year after being convicted of conspiring to bribe a federal judge. In 1933 he told his life-story to Upton Sinclair who published it himself as a personal attack on the movie industry and as a piece of special pleading by Fox, under the title *Upton Sinclair Presents William Fox* (Los Angeles, 1933).

Biographical Notes

WILLIAM GOETZ (1903–   )

Born in New York, educated at Pennsylvania College. Producer at M-G-M and Paramount in the 1920s, and with Fox Films from 1930 when he married Louis B. Mayer's elder daughter, Edith. Became a producer at the newly formed Twentieth Century Company in 1933 and vice-president of Twentieth Century-Fox on merger, and in 1942-3 was in charge of production. In 1943 he formed International Films, which merged with Universal Pictures in 1946. He was executive-in-charge-of-production at Universal-International until the 'fifties when he became an independent producer at Warner Brothers, Columbia, etc. His elder brother Ben also worked for M-G-M and was head of M-G-M productions in Great Britain.

SAMUEL GOLDWYN (1882–   )

Born in Warsaw. Worked as an office boy before running away from home at the age of eleven. Got to England where he lived with relatives in Manchester (serving as blacksmith's assistant), before travelling on to America at the age of fifteen. Apprenticed in glove factory before opening his own successful business. In 1913, partially influenced by the threat to the glove trade through President Wilson's lifting of import tariffs on foreign leather, he formed Lasky Feature Plays with his brother-in-law Jesse Lasky and DeMille. Left Famous Players-Lasky shortly after merger, and in 1916 joined the Selwyn brothers in the Goldwyn Picture Corp., changing his name from Goldfish to Goldwyn in 1918. In the same year the company moved from Fort Lee, New Jersey, to Culver City outside Los Angeles. Goldwyn broke with the Selwyns in 1919, returned eighteen months later and finally quit in 1922. Played no part in the M-G-M merger and founded his own company after being bought out. (In 1925, having been divorced from Blanche Lasky, he married actress Frances Howard.) Goldwyn was then Hollywood's major independent producer until his virtual retirement in the late 'fifties (last production *Porgy and Bess,* 1959) owning his own studio, having stars under contract, personally supervising and financing his pictures, and releasing them through United Artists and RKO. Published his own vague memoir of Hollywood in 1923 (*Behind the Screen*). A short, wry, generally adulatory biography was written in 1937 by Alva Johnston of the *New Yorker*, (*The Great Goldwyn*, Random House, New York, 1937), and a study of his movies by Richard Griffith, *Samuel Goldwyn, the Producer and his Films* (New York, the Museum of Modern Art Film Library, 1956).

WILL H. HAYS (1879–1954)

Born in Sullivan, Indiana, son of a local lawyer and Presbyterian elder whose family firm he entered after studying at Wabash College. An active figure in local, and later national, Republican politics. National chairman at the Republican Party's Convention in 1920 when Warren Harding was nominated as presidential candidate. After Harding's election victory Hays became Postmaster General and in 1921 was invited to become the first president of the newly formed Motion Picture Producers and Distributors of America (MPPDA), subsequently named MPAA (14 December 1945). Hays was succeeded in 1945 by Eric A. Johnston (1895-1963), a banker, businessman, and wartime Roosevelt aide, who for a number of years had been a director and president of the US Chamber of Commerce. The post is now held by the Texan Jack Valenti (b. 1921), former key adviser to Lyndon Johnson. Hays told his own story with characteristic dourness in *The Memoirs of Will H. Hays*, published posthumously (New York, Doubleday, 1955).

WILLIAM RANDOLPH HEARST (1863–1950)

Born in San Francisco, the only son of a self-made mining millionaire who became senator for California, and his strong-willed wife, a Presbyterian schoolmistress from Missouri. Educated at Harvard (expelled for practical joking); entered journalism with father's *San Francisco Examiner*, bought the *New York Journal* in 1895, and established political influence through a chain of newspapers and magazines. Made several unsuccessful bids for presidency, Senate, and New York governorship, served two terms in Washington as Representative from New York City. Married Millicent Wilson in 1903. Entered movies in 1912 with newsreels; his International Film Service was making serials by 1915. His personal interest in the cinema was heightened in 1917 when Marion Davies, a Ziegfeld Follies girl and daughter of a minor New York politician, became his life-long mistress. From 1919 onwards his Cosmopolitan Pictures, assisted by publicity in his newspapers, were principally devoted to making Miss Davies a major star. In 1924, after Cosmopolitan's New York City studio was burnt down, the company moved to California, where it was eventually installed at M-G-M's Culver City studio until 1934 when it transferred to Warner Brothers. Throughout the 'twenties and 'thirties Hearst was the cynosure of Hollywood, and his parties, especially at his beach house and his mansion San Simeon, were the highlights of the film colony's social life. While remaining a wealthy man he underwent a spectacular decline in his fortune in the late 'thirties due to his extravagant living and had to divest himself of newspapers, property, and his vast art collection.

Hearst was the inspiration for Joseph Stoyte in Aldous Huxley's novel *After Many a Summer* (1939), and for Orson Welles's film *Citizen Kane* (1941), and is the subject of numerous studies, most notably W. A. Swanberg's fine *Citizen Hearst* (New York, Scribners, 1961; London, Longmans Green, 1962).

HOWARD HUGHES (1905–   )

Born in Houston, Texas. Son of a Harvard-educated lawyer and businessman who had invented a highly profitable roller bit for hard surface drilling in the oil industry. Inherited the multimillion dollar Hughes Tool Co. at eighteen, on his father's death, and developed it into one of the world's largest aircraft and electronics complexes. Mechanical genius, aviation record holder, plane designer and creator of Trans-World Airlines. Came to Hollywood initially with his father and returned in the late 'twenties as an independent producer. Directed *Hell's Angels*

(1930), *The Outlaw* (1943), etc. In 1948 he acquired RKO which he ran until 1957 before selling out to television interests. Since then he has played little part in the film industry, living as a recluse with his ex-film star wife Jean Peters (whom he married secretly in 1957), latterly in Las Vegas where he has steadily become the largest single real estate owner. He is the subject of two well-documented, wholly unauthorized biographies: *Howard Hughes* by John Keats (New York, Random House, 1966; London, MacGibbon and Kee, 1967); and *The Bashful Billionaire* by Albert B. Gerber (New York, Lyle Stuart, 1967). He was also the remote model for Jonas Cord Jr in Harold Robbins's repellent novel *The Carpetbaggers* (1961).

SAM KATZ (1892–   )

Came with Russian parents to Chicago at the age of three months. Father a barber. At twelve he was a two-dollar-a-week messenger boy, then a switchboard repairer and, at thirteen, a pianist in Carl Laemmle's first nickelodeon, while working his way through school and college. Owned three theatres while still a teenager. Built up a cinema chain which he merged with fellow Chicagoan Barney Balaban's chain to become one of the largest exhibitors in the midwest. In 1925 Katz and Balaban joined forces with Paramount-Famous-Lasky, where until 1932 Katz was in charge of theatres and vice-president. (Balaban remained with Paramount to become president in 1935.) After a spell with his own company, Producing Artists, Katz was hired in 1936 by Nicholas Schenck as an M-G-M vice-president in Hollywood, with special responsibility for B-features and later musicals. Like the Irish M-G-M executive Eddie Mannix, Katz was sent out by Schenck as a countervailing force to Mayer and, like Mannix, became a Mayer ally. In 1950 he became chairman of the board of Stanley Kramer's independent production company which released its movies first through United Artists and then through Columbia.

JOSEPH P. KENNEDY (1888–   )

Grandson of a poor Irish immigrant and the son of a prosperous saloon keeper, who became a state senator. Graduated from Harvard in 1912 and entered business via position as state banking examiner (gained through father's influence). Married in 1914 the daughter of Boston's mayor John F. Fitzgerald. Had nine children, including the late President John F. Kennedy and the late Senator Robert J. Kennedy. Acquired interest in New England cinema chain after the first world war, and in 1926 bought Film Booking Office of America Inc. from British owners and moved to New York. Personally supervised production, specializing in second features, in Hollywood, and arranged for movie moguls to deliver a series of lectures at Harvard Business School, subsequently published with an introduction by himself as *The Story of the Films* (Chicago, A. W. Shaw, 1927). During the period of consolidation at the time of the arrival of the talkies he ruthlessly masterminded a complex series of mergers involving his own FBO, the Keith-Albee and Orpheum chains, and the movie interests of General Electric, Westinghouse Electric and the Radio Corporation of America, that led to the formation of the vast RKO Radio organization. Kennedy, after quitting the cinema, devoted himself to banking and democratic politics (serving as ambassador to the Court of St James 1938-40). From time to time he acted in an advisory capacity to the industry; in 1937 he was author of a devastating report on the mismanagement of Paramount which was never officially released. There is a first class biography by Richard J. Whalen, *The Founding Father* (New York, New American Library, 1964; London, Hutchinson, 1964).

SIDNEY KENT (1886-1942)

Born in Lincoln, Nebraska; started life as a manual labourer on Nebraska railroads and Milwaukee docks; by the age of twenty he was a minor executive with Colorado Fuel and Iron Company in Wyoming and subsequently a salesman for the American Druggists' Syndicate and, his first film job, the Vitagraph Company. After assisting in the winding-up of the Patent Company's General Film Company he joined Famous Players-Lasky and became general manager of Paramount. In 1932, with a major reputation as a sales executive (he was called 'the father of the motion picture sales convention'), he was invited by the bankers to become executive vice-president, and two weeks later president, of the reorganized Fox company, a position he retained until his death in 1942, when Spyros Skouras succeeded him.

CARL LAEMMLE (1867–1939)

Born at Laupheim, Germany, the tenth of a poor Jewish estate agent's thirteen children. Left school at thirteen and after serving as an apprentice in a relative's store, he emigrated to America in 1884 to join his brother in Chicago. Did numerous clerical jobs in clothing and jewellery trades and in stock yards, before moving in 1894 to Oshkosh, Wisconsin, as book-keeper for the Continental Clothing Co. of whose local store he became manager after marrying the owner's niece in 1898. In 1905 he resigned when refused a rise in pay, and in 1906, while looking for a Chicago site for his own store, decided to open a nickelodeon, the famous Whitefront Theatre. A chain of cinemas was followed by a movie distribution business, the Laemmle Film Service. In 1909 he stood out against the Patent Company, fighting them in the courts, ridiculing them in the press, and competing with them by producing his own movies. His Independent Motion Picture Co. (IMP) was the principal element in an anti-Patent Co. grouping that in 1912 became the Universal Company. Produced from two small studios in Los Angeles until 1915 when Universal City, then California's largest studio, was opened in San Fernando Valley. Much of his time in the 1920s was taken up with philanthropic work, particularly over relief for Germany. In 1929 he appointed his son (Carl Laemmle Jr, b. 1908) general manager in charge of production. In 1936 he was forced out of the ailing company by banking interests, and his son, who had been responsible for – among other significant films – *All Quiet on the Western*

Front and *Frankenstein,* left too, to work as an independent producer. In 1930 John Drinkwater was commissioned to write a biography of Laemmle, a project apparently not wholly unconnected with a fantastic bid for the Nobel Peace Prize, and the sympathetic, uncritical result was published as *The Life and Adventures of Carl Laemmle* (London, Heinemann, 1931).

JESSE L. LASKY (1880–1958)

San Francisco-born son of a failed shoe-seller and grandson of a German immigrant who had crossed the continent in 1848. Professional cornet player with travelling medicine show and, after abortive participation in Alaskan goldrush, with an orchestra in Hawaii. On his return he was joined by sister Blanche in cornet duo act, touring America and Europe before settling down in the east and gradually moving into vaudeville management and production. Married in 1908 the daughter of a Russian immigrant in Boston. Lost a hundred thousand dollars in 1912 in an attempt to launch the Folies Bergères restaurant in New York. In 1913 founded Jesse Lasky Feature Plays with Blanche's husband Samuel Goldwyn, Arthur S. Friend and Cecil B. DeMille, and on the merger with Zukor's Famous Players became vice-president in charge of production at what was later called Paramount. He held this position, supervising the Hollywood and Long Island studios, until 1932 when he was forced out of the company, a virtual bankrupt as a result of the fall in value of Paramount stock. Joined Sidney Kent as producer at Fox for three years, then with Mary Pickford at United Artists as president of the short-lived Pickford-Lasky Corporation. From 1938 to 1940 he produced the radio talent-spotting programme 'Gateway to Hollywood'. Returned to the cinema in 1941 as producer at Warner Brothers and then at RKO and M-G-M. In 1957, heavily in debt to the inland revenue, he came back to Paramount to prepare a long-contemplated project *The Big Brass Band* with the assistance of DeMille and a long-estranged Goldwyn, who promised adequate finance a few days before Lasky's death. His son Jesse Jr achieved some reputation as a screenwriter, particularly through scripts for DeMille epics. Lasky wrote (with Don Weldon) a breezy, very guarded autobiography, *I Blow My Own Horn* (New York, Doubleday, 1957; London, Gollancz, 1957).

MARCUS LOEW (1870-1927)

Born on Manhattan's lower East Side, son of an Austrian immigrant waiter. Sold newspapers at six, left school at nine to work as a map colourer, salesman of advertising sheets, and then at twelve in a fur factory. Independent fur broker at eighteen, broke at nineteen, recovered and, after being married in 1894, had a second business failure from which he again made a come-back. In 1899, Loew went into theatrical real estate and in 1904 followed his friend Adolph Zukor into arcade and nickelodeon business. Built up vaudeville and legitimate theatre business in collaboration with Joe and Nicholas Schenck and Adolph Zukor, which in 1910 became Loew's Consolidated Enterprises; and in 1919, much enlarged with a vast movie chain and a nine and a half million dollars bank loan, it became Loew's Inc. Loew had never opposed the Patent Company and did not enter production until 1920 when he bought the Metro company for three million dollars and in 1924 merged it with the Goldwyn and Mayer companies. In the 1920s his son Arthur Loew, the then husband of Adolph Zukor's daughter, superintended the corporation's extensive overseas expansion. In 1923 he suffered a heart attack, and died in 1927 at his Long Island mansion after a period of illness, leaving a personal fortune exceeding thirty million dollars.

LOUIS B. MAYER (1885-1957)

Born in Russia, he came to America as a child with parents who settled in St John's, Nova Scotia, where his father, a Hebraic scholar, worked as a scrap collector and junk dealer. Joined his father in the business at the age of eight, and at nineteen moved to Boston, set up his own junk business and married the daughter of a local butcher and cantor. Had two daughters who married producers William Goetz and David Selznick. Bought first movie house in Haverhill, Mass., in 1907, and gradually built up in partnership a chain of cinemas and legitimate theatres that extended from Canada to Pennsylvania. Made rich by local franchise of *Birth of a Nation* and entered production with Alco Company (later Metro pictures) which he left in 1917. Started personal production with a hired Brooklyn studio in 1918 and moved to a studio in Los Angeles. In 1924 he became production head at M-G-M's Culver City studio after the merger with Metro and Goldwyn's companies, a position he held until he reluctantly resigned in 1951. For several years in the 'thirties and 'forties he was the highest salaried individual in the United States. He was active in Republican politics (California state chairman). Created one of America's largest racing stables, which he sold in 1947. The same year he was divorced and married a dancer, Lorena Danker, thirty years his junior. Mayer was responsible for founding the Academy of Motion Picture Arts and Sciences in 1927 as a company union to combat the threatened unionization of actors and directors. From 1951 to 1954 he was adviser to the Cinerama corporation and then spent his last three years intriguing with stockholders to eject top officials at Loew's Inc.

Mayer is the subject of an excellent biography by Bosley Crowther, *Hollywood Rajah* (New York, Holt, Rinehart and Winston, 1960); and a partial model for Brady in Fitzgerald's *The Last Tycoon*.

DORE SCHARY (1905–   )

Born at Newark, New Jersey, and first worked as an entertainer during vacation jobs as a waiter in Jewish holiday camps in the Catskills, before becoming professional actor, journalist and unsuccessful playwright. Joined Columbia as scriptwriter in 1932, then worked on free-lance or short contract basis for Universal, M-G-M, Fox and Warner, winning Best Original Screenplay Oscar for *Boys' Town* in 1938. In 1942 he headed his own low-budget production unit at M-G-M which he quit the following year after the studio's refusal to film his allegorical Western *Storm in the West* (written with Sinclair Lewis and published in book form in 1963). Joined David O. Selznick's Vanguard pictures and was later lent as producer to RKO, where in 1947 he became head of production. Quarrelled with Howard Hughes and returned to M-G-M as vice-president in charge of production in 1948, and then as head of the studio in 1951 after Mayer's resignation. Dismissed in 1956 during studio upheaval. Returned to Broadway as producer and author (e.g. *Sunrise at Campobello*, 1958) with occasional unimpressive forays into independent film production.

In 1950 he published *Case History of a Movie* (New York, Random House), an informative account of the filming at M-G-M of his pretentious inspirational picture *The Next Voice You Hear*.

JOSEPH M. SCHENCK (1877–1961)

Came to New York from Russia in the late 1880s with his parents and brother Nicholas (1881-1969). Like several other moguls born abroad, the Schencks have been rather cagey about their birth dates. Nick was very likely born in 1881, though he didn't reveal the date for professional directories, preferring to describe himself as having come 'to US at 9'. Joe always gave his birthday as 25 December 1882 which made him appear the younger and records that he 'came to US with parents at an early age'; but he was almost certainly born five years earlier. In consequence there are considerable discrepancies as to Joe's age in his obituaries. Some aspects of the brothers' first quarter of a century in America are also clouded in mystery which, as with a number of their peers, may be just as well. Unquestionably they both obtained some minor qualifications as pharmacists, worked in and ran drug-stores in the Bronx, before acquiring an amusement park in north Manhattan and later in New Jersey. The brothers leased film concessions in these parks to Marcus Loew and then joined the Loew organization where another brother was a theatre manager. Nick became secretary of Loew's Consolidated in 1910 and Joe ran the group's theatres. Joe left in 1917 to produce his own films for Lewis Selznick's company with his wife Norma Talmadge as star and also guided the fortunes of Buster Keaton, husband of Natalie Talmadge. Subsequently he was with First National, president of United Artists (whose small circuit of preview cinemas he organized and remained associated with for nearly thirty years), and in 1933 founded Twentieth Century with Darryl Zanuck (with a loan from Nick who in 1927 had succeeded Loew as president of Loew's Inc.). On the merger with Fox, he became chairman of Twentieth Century-Fox. In 1941 Joe was gaoled for a year in an income tax and Union pay-off scandal and served four months; he was pardoned and his lost citizenship restored by President Harry Truman in 1947. In December 1955, Nick Schenck was succeeded as president of Loew's Inc. by Arthur Loew (son of the founder) and became chairman of the board; the following year saw his elevation to honorary chairman and within a matter of months he retired. In 1952 Joe received a special Academy Award for 'long and distinguished service' to the industry, left Fox and in 1953 joined the late Mike Todd in the Magna Corporation to explore widescreen techniques (a development notably neglected by his cautious brother). The latter years of Joe's life were dogged by illness and he was inactive from the mid-fifties until his death.

B. P. SCHULBERG (1892–1957)

Born in Bridgeport, Connecticut. A reporter with the New York *Evening Mail* before joining Rex Pictures as publicity director and scenarist (Rex was an independent – i.e. outlaw – company that handled the pictures of director Edwin S. Porter and actress Gloria Swanson), and then Adolph Zukor's Famous Players, where he worked on the publicity of *Queen Elizabeth* in 1912. He left Famous Players-Lasky after the first world war to become an independent producer (releasing through United Artists), during which period he discovered Clara Bow, the 'It' Girl, and in 1922 briefly shared the primitive Los Angeles studio of his one-time friend, Louis B. Mayer. He rejoined Zukor's company in 1925 and became general manager of Paramount's West Coast studio, a position from which he was ousted in 1932. For several years he was again an independent, before working as a producer for a number of companies including Columbia and Selznick International. For most of the post-war years until his death, he was unemployed despite an expensive 1949 advertising campaign in the trade press to draw attention to his availability. The short, tough, aggressive Ben Schulberg is best known as the father of the sensitive, stammering novelist Budd Schulberg (1914–   ), screenwriter, sports journalist and author of several novels, most notably his Hollywood books, *What Makes Sammy Run?* and *The Disenchanted.*

DAVID O. SELZNICK (1902–65)

Born in Pittsburgh. Son of Kiev-born jewellery salesman and movie pioneer Lewis J. Selznick, whose production company failed in 1923 and who died in 1932. Like his elder brother Myron (who became a successful actors' agent and died in 1944), David was trained by his father and made his own way in films, first with quickie documentaries and, after failures in publishing and Florida real estate, as producer in Hollywood: with M-G-M (1926–30), Paramount, and RKO (as head of production), then M-G-M, as a vice-president, until 1935 when he established his own independent company, Selznick International, to release through United Artists and later through his own distribution company. In 1939 he made his most important film *Gone With the Wind* (released through M-G-M). He had only one major post-war success, *Duel in the Sun* (1947) and many flops, including his last picture *A Farewell to Arms* (1957). In 1930 he married Louis B. Mayer's younger daughter Irene (divorced 1948) and in 1949 actress Jennifer Jones.

WINFIELD R. SHEEHAN (1883–1945)

Born in Buffalo, N.Y., the son of Irish-American Catholic parents, and educated locally at the Roman Catholic St Canisius College. Began a career in journalism as a cub reporter in Buffalo, and in 1902 moved to New York as police reporter on the New York *World.* In 1910 became secretary to the New York fire commissioner and shortly after secretary to police commissioner Rhinelander Waldo. During this period he was involved in several police graft cases, but never indicted, and came into contact with the film industry and especially William Fox for whose fight with the Patent Company he provided strong-arm men and valuable political influence. In 1914 he went to work full-time for Fox as a hundred-dollar-a-week personal secretary; in 1916 he was made Fox Company's vice-president and general manager at twenty thousand dollars a year. Became head of production at Fox's Hollywood studios and was noted, even among fellow moguls, for the opulent style in which he and his wife, the former opera star Maria Jeritza, lived at their million dollar Beverly Hills mansion and San Fernando Valley retreat. He was abroad nursing a liver complaint in 1929 during the Fox panic but on his return was encouraged (according to Fox, by the inveterate go-between A. C. Blumenthal) to desert his master and join the new management as head of production at 250,000 dollars a year rising to 500,000 dollars in his fifth year. In 1935 he resigned on the merger of the Twentieth Century Company with Fox, but returned to production in 1939 to make *Florian* at M-G-M, and again in 1943 to produce *Captain Eddie,* a film biography of the aviator Eddie Rickenbacker, at Twentieth Century-Fox. The latter film was due to be released the week he died, in August 1945.

SPYROS P. SKOURAS (1895–   )

Born in extreme poverty in Skourohorian, Greece, Emigrated to America with his younger brothers Charles and George in 1908, settling in St Louis where they worked as newsvendors, waiters and hotel bell-boys. They opened their first cinema in 1914 which was developed into an important middle-western circuit, which they sold to Warner Brothers and continued to manage along with the other Warner cinemas. Spyros joined Paramount in 1931 to supervise Paramount theatres, and the following year moved with his brothers into the Fox cinemas which they ran alongside their own theatre chain. Charles and George remained in cinema management, but in 1942 on the death of Sidney Kent, Spyros became president of Twentieth Century-Fox. Spyros' Yale-educated sons (Plato and Spyros S.) joined him in the business. Inside the industry Spyros is most celebrated for the introduction of CinemaScope at Twentieth Century-Fox in 1953 (for which the company received a special Academy Award 'in recognition of their imagination, showmanship and foresight'). The Skouras family were all active in the Greek War Relief Association during the second world war. After the return of Darryl Zanuck in 1962, Spyros became the uninfluential chairman of Twentieth Century-Fox; later he sold his sizeable interest in the company and devoted himself to running a fleet of oil tankers, an activity befitting a Greek millionaire.

Skouras: King of Fox Studios by Carlo Curti (Los Angeles, Holloway House, 1967) is a garbled, totally unreliable life of Spyros.

IRVING THALBERG (1899–1936)

Son of a middle-class Brooklyn lace importer. Joined Universal's New York office as a clerk in 1917; went to Hollywood in 1919 as Carl Laemmle's secretary and was left in charge of the studio a few months later. At one point he was rumoured to be the fiancé of Laemmle's daughter. Joined Louis B. Mayer in 1923 and became Mayer's second-in-command on the formation of M-G-M the following year. In 1927 he married Norma Shearer whose brother Douglas was head of M-G-M's sound department and a considerable technical innovator. Thalberg's brother-in-law Lawrence Weingarten produced M-G-M's first *all*-talking picture, *The Broadway Melody*. General poor health culminating in heart trouble took him away from the studios for some months in 1933. He was never well again after his return and he died in 1936. His plans to enter independent production had been delayed by Loew's Inc. president Nicholas Schenck's refusal to release him from contract. In 1937 a new Oscar for distinguished production, The Irving Thalberg Memorial Award, was created.

Thalberg was the model for Miles Calman in Scott Fitzgerald's short story *Crazy Sunday* (1932) and for Monroe Stahr in Fitzgerald's uncompleted novel *The Last Tycoon* (1941).

HAL B. WALLIS (1889–   )

Born in Chicago, he first entered films in the early 1920s on the exhibition side, managing a Los Angeles cinema, before joining the publicity department at Warner Brothers. Worked on publicity for *The Jazz Singer* in 1927. Became an executive producer under Warner's production chief Darryl Zanuck whom he succeeded in 1933. In 1938 and 1943 he received the Irving Thalberg Memorial Award. Set up Hal Wallis Productions to make his own films at Warner Brothers in 1944, and moved this independent operation to Paramount in 1947 where it has remained.

WALTER WANGER (1894–1968)

Born Walter Feuchtwanger, son of a wealthy San Francisco businessman; educated at Dartmouth College. Worked in New York and London theatre until he was brought into movies in the early 'twenties by Jesse Lasky, initially to buy plays for Paramount and discover talent from the theatre. Subsequently a Paramount producer, then a producer with M-G-M and Columbia vice-president before an extensive career as independent producer, releasing through United Artists and RKO. Served a four-month gaol sentence in 1952 for armed assault on the agent of his wife, the film star Joan Bennett, but came back to movies as a producer at Allied Artists, making *Riot in Cell Block Eleven* (1954), an attack on American prison conditions, and other small budget films. (Allied Artists was a wholly owned subsidiary of the now defunct B-feature factory Monogram Pictures, set up to turn out higher quality movies than the usual Monogram offerings. It was with Allied Artists that the now highly influential independent producers Harold and Walter Mirisch got their first production experience.) In the late fifties Wanger returned to major production with *I Want to Live* and *Cleopatra*; the latter agonizing experience at Twentieth Century-Fox is recorded in his book, written with Jo Hyams, *My Life with Cleopatra* (New York, Bantam Books; London, Corgi Books, 1963). Wanger was the producer who took Budd Schulberg and Scott Fitzgerald on the disastrous trip to Dartmouth in 1939, the event that inspired Schulberg's novel *The Disenchanted* (1951).

WARNER BROTHERS

Sons of a cobbler, Ben Warner, from Kraznashiltz, Poland, who arrived in the United States with his wife and eldest son Harry (1881-1958) in 1883 to set up shop in Baltimore, where Albert Warner (1884-1967) was born. Ben subsequently travelled as a pedlar during which time Sam Warner (1888-1927) and Jack L. Warner (1892-   ) were born, the latter in London, Ontario. The family finally settled in Youngstown, Ohio, where Harry had first opened a cobbler's shop, which Ben developed as a general store and butcher's. Sam worked as an ice-cream salesman, fairground barker, and on the railroad; the others were also salesmen, Harry selling meat and Albert selling soap, before running a bicycle shop together. In 1904 they bought a film projector and gave travelling shows, beginning at Niles, Ohio, with sister Rose playing the piano and twelve-year-old Jack singing as boy soprano. They ran the ninety-seat Cascades cinema at Newcastle, Pennsylvania, from 1905 to 1907 when they moved into film distribution in Pittsburgh with branches in Maryland and Georgia. Sold out to Patent Company, and returned to exhibition in 1910 with a road show of *Dante's Inferno*. In 1912 Jack and Sam went to California, where they set up movie exchanges and tried their hand unsuccessfully at production, until after war service the brothers made their first successful film in 1919. Under the present company title Warner Brothers was incorporated in 1923 and bought its first cinema, back home in Youngstown, the following year. The company rapidly expanded, especially after the successful experiments with sound which began in 1925 in association with Western Electric and culminated in the August 1926 showing of *Don Juan* (with recorded musical accompaniment) at the Warner Cinema on

Broadway, and *The Jazz Singer*, premièred 6 October 1927, twenty-four hours after the death of Sam Warner who had supervised the sound campaign. (The initial aim of the Warner Brothers sound – which was the soon discarded synchronized disc system – was not to bring speech to pictures but to make full orchestral accompaniment available to more cinemas and for all performances. *The Jazz Singer* became a talking film virtually by accident.) The company absorbed, among others, the Vitagraph and First National companies, together with their cinemas and exchanges, and established their permanent studio at Burbank outside Los Angeles, with Jack as vice-president in charge of production and Harry and Albert in New York as president and treasurer, where they remained until Albert's retirement in 1956 and Harry's death. The brothers resisted several stockholders' attempts to unseat them and were known in the early 'thirties to have dispensed with company stock and taken debentures to avoid being hit by the depression. Jack Warner continued into the late 'sixties as head of production, personally producing *My Fair Lady* and *Camelot*, and retained his own independent unit after Warner Brothers was taken over by Seven Arts, as well as becoming president of Warner Brothers-Seven Arts Studio and vice-chairman of the Warner Brothers-Seven Arts Board. Jack has written with Dean Jennings a lively, cocky and unreliable autobiography, *My First Hundred Years in Hollywood* (New York, Random House, 1965). Several ex-employees of Warner Brothers have pointed out that Dean Jennings also helped the warden of San Quentin, California's State penitentiary, to write his memoirs.

DARRYL FRANCIS ZANUCK (1902–   )

Born at Wahoo, Nebraska; his Methodist father was a hotel clerk of Swiss parentage from Iowa, his mother a Nebraskan of English stock. When his parents separated, he moved with his mother to Los Angeles. After war service in France with the Nebraska National Guard he returned to California and worked as a newspaper subscription salesman, shipyard labourer, poster tinter in theatre lobbies, and then screenwriter with Warner Brothers where he became a producer and in 1929 head of production. Married actress Virginia Fox in 1924. Left Warners in 1933 and started Twentieth Century Picture Company with Joseph Schenck and was vice-president in charge of production of Twentieth Century-Fox (with a short wartime break during which he was a lieutenant-colonel in the Signal Corps, making documentary films) until 1956 when he became an independent producer releasing through Fox. In 1962 he returned from his Paris base to New York to wrest from Spyros Skouras the presidency of Twentieth Century-Fox, a position he still holds. His son Richard (b. Los Angeles 1934), formerly an independent producer and assistant producer for his father's own company, is head of production at Fox's Hollywood studio.

ADOLPH ZUKOR (1873–   )

Born in Ricse, Hungary; his father, an impoverished store-keeper-farmer, died when Adolph was a year old. Lived with his uncle and was apprenticed as a clerk, until emigrating to the United States in 1889. Worked as a furrier's apprentice and then with his own fur business in New York and Chicago where he designed a new style clasp for neck-pieces. Finally settled near friend and fellow furrier Marcus Loew in New York. In 1903 entered the penny arcade business with branches the following year in Newark, Philadelphia and Boston; in 1904 he opened Crystal Hall, a (for the time) semi-palatial cinema on 14th Street, New York. Merged interests with Marcus Loew in Loew's Consolidated, of which he was treasurer. Left Loew in 1912 to launch Engadine Corp. to show imported film of *Queen Elizabeth* starring Sarah Bernhardt, for the completion of which he had put up some money. After the première of *Queen Elizabeth* (12 July 1912) he conceived the idea of Famous Players in Famous Plays and made a series of movies, in defiance of the Patent Company, starring stage actors in their current successes, directed by his partner Edwin S. Porter initially in a New York warehouse. At the same time he signed up Mary Pickford for productions in

Hollywood. Merged Famous Players with Jesse L. Lasky Feature Plays in 1916 with himself as president, Lasky vice-president, Sam Goldwyn chairman and DeMille director general. In 1919 he got a ten million dollar bank loan to begin an extensive programme of theatre acquisition which continued until the end of the 'twenties. In 1917 he also became head of Famous Players-Lasky's distributing company, Paramount, which was eventually consolidated with the production company and cinema chain. Zukor survived attempts by creditors to push him out during Paramount's period in receivership in the early 'thirties, but in 1935 was made chairman of the board and replaced as president by Barney Balaban. Returned briefly to Hollywood for a period of active production in 1937, but was otherwise mainly in New York from around 1917 and increasingly from the late 'thirties a figurehead, though with considerable influence, finishing up as a nonagenarian chairman-of-the-board emeritus. His autobiography *The Public is Never Wrong* (New York, G. P. Putnam, 1953; London, Cassell, 1953), written with Dale Kramer, contains useful information but is not especially revealing and something less than frank.

BIBLIOGRAPHY

Apart from the books mentioned in the biographical notes, the following are of interest:

Anger, Kenneth, *Hollywood Babylon* (Phoenix, Associated Professional Services, 1965). Scabrous, shamefully fascinating, uncensorious and unreliable history of movie scandals.

Bessie, Alvah, *Inquisition in Eden* (New York, Macmillan, 1965; East Berlin, Seven Seas Books, 1967). Autobiography of a left-wing novelist and screenwriter who was one of the 'Hollywood Ten'. Moving and somewhat ingenuous.

Blesh, Rudi, *Keaton* (London, Secker and Warburg, 1967). A detailed biography based on extensive interviews with Buster Keaton. Contains valuable material on Joseph Schenck and M-G-M.

Brodsky, Jack and Nathan Weiss, *The Cleopatra Papers* (New York, Simon and Schuster, 1963). Frank, amusing exchange of letters between two Twentieth Century-Fox publicists during the filming of *Cleopatra*.

Brownlow, Kevin, *The Parade's Gone By* (New York, Knopf, 1968; London, Secker and Warburg, 1968). A long, well-informed and exceedingly interesting study of the American silent cinema based almost entirely on interview material recorded by the author with important survivors of the period.

Chaplin, Charles, *My Autobiography* (New York, Simon and Schuster; London, The Bodley Head, 1964).

Cogley, John, *Report on Blacklisting I – The Movies* (New York, Fund for the Republic, 1956). A judicious, meticulously documented book on politics and the film industry in the post-war decade. An extremely lively chapter on Hollywood's left-wing politics is 'The Day of the Locust' in Murray Kempton's scintillating interpretation of the American left – a look at 'some monuments and ruins of the 'thirties' – called *Part of Our Time* (New York, Simon and Schuster, 1955).

Crowther, Bosley, *The Lion's Share* (New York, Dutton, 1957). A first-class history of Loew's Inc. and M-G-M by the biographer of Louis B. Mayer, but not a critique of the studio's movies.

Goodman, Ezra, *The Fifty-Year Decline and Fall of Hollywood* (New York, Simon and Schuster, 1961). A lengthy, cynical, anecdote-packed account of all aspects of the business by a former studio publicist and *Time* reporter, who knows and loathes the industry.

Goodman, Walter, *The Committee* (New York, Farrar, Strauss and Giroux, 1968; London, Secker and Warburg, 1969). A history of the House Committee on Un-American Activities since its inception in 1938, but dealing in less detail with the film industry than Cogley's *Report on Blacklisting*.

Griffith, Richard and Arthur Mayer, *The Movies* (New York, Simon and Schuster, 1957; London, Spring Books, 1963). An admirable pictorial history of the American cinema.

Hall, Ben M., *The Best Remaining Seats* (New York, Bramhall House, 1961). A beautifully produced, affectionately written history of the great period of American cinema construction and management.

Hampton, Benjamin B. *A History of the Movies* (New York, Covici and Friede, 1931). An important industrial history from the turn of the century by a man who was intimately involved in the commercial side of film-making.

Hecht, Ben, *A Child of the Century* (New York, Simon and Schuster, 1954). The brilliant, racy autobiography of the journalist and playwright who became Hollywood's highest paid screenwriter.

Jacobs, Lewis, *The Rise of the American Film* (New York, Harcourt Brace, 1939). An indispensable work that has never unfortunately been brought up to date. An unrevised, uncorrected paperback edition accompanied by an essay on 'Ex-

perimental Cinema in America 1921-47' was published by
Teachers College Press, New York, in 1968.

Jobes, Gertrude, *Motion Picture Empire* (Hampton, Conn.,
Archon Books, 1966). A not entirely successful attempt to
make intelligible the tortuous financial affairs of the American
cinema, but contains much invaluable information.

Kahn, Gordon, *Hollywood on Trial* (New York, Boni and Gaer,
1948). A polemical book, written by a deeply involved left-
wing screenwriter, about Hollywood politics and the HUAC
inquiries. A disingenuous work for the most part but of considerable historical and documentary value to the careful reader.

Knight, Arthur, *The Liveliest Art* (New York, Macmillan,
1957). Amongst the best single volume introductions to the
cinema which set the American film industry in a world context.

MacCann, Richard Dyer, *Hollywood in Transition* (Boston,
Houghton, Mifflin, 1962). Uneven collection of articles on contemporary Hollywood by a *Christian Science Monitor* correspondent.

Macgowan, Kenneth, *Behind the Screen* (New York, Delacorte
Press, 1965). A rambling book that tries to cover too much
ground, but the author brings to the task his experience as a
drama critic, teacher, and, for fifteen years, a producer at
RKO and Twentieth Century-Fox.

Mayersberg, Paul, *Hollywood the Haunted House* (London,
Allen Lane The Penguin Press, 1967). A young British writer's
personal impressions of life and working conditions in present-
day Hollywood, with extensive interview material.

Oppenheimer, George, *The View from the Sixties* (New York,
David McKay, 1966). Witty, light-weight autobiography by a
critic and playwright who spent many years in Hollywood
working mainly for M-G-M.

Powdermaker, Hortense, *Hollywood the Dream Factory* (Boston,
Little Brown, 1950; London, Secker and Warburg, 1951).
An anthropological approach to Hollywood by a noted former
pupil of Malinowski. Dr Powdermaker has described the background to her field work in Hollywood and elsewhere in

Stranger and Friend, The Way of an Anthropologist (London, Secker and Warburg, 1967).

Ramsaye, Terry, *A Million and One Nights* (New York, Simon and Schuster, 1926; London, Frank Cass, 1964). The classic pioneering history of the American cinema; now very dated but worth reading for the author's personal style alone.

Robinson, David, *Hollywood in the Twenties* (London, Zwemmer; New York, A. S. Barnes, 1968). A well-written paperback that combines industrial history with criticism; the first of three useful volumes – the other two are John Baxter's *Hollywood in the Thirties* and Charles Higham and Joel Greenberg's *Hollywood in the Forties*.

Ross, Lillian, *Picture* (New York, Rinehart, 1952; London, Gollancz, 1952). Devastating objective report on the making of John Huston's film *The Red Badge of Courage* at M-G-M from initial conception to final exhibition.

Rosten, Leo, *Hollywood: The Movie Colony, the Movie Makers* (New York, Harcourt Brace, 1941). Based on three years research by a team of economists and sociologists, this is by far the best written, most fully documented book on Hollywood in its industrial prime.

Schumach, Murray, *The Face on the Cutting Room Floor* (New York, William Morrow, 1964). An informal history of all forms of film censorship and outside pressures on Hollywood. Entertaining, but poorly documented and not entirely reliable. Historically useful but now rather dated American books on censorship are: *Freedom of the Movies* by Ruth A. Inglis (Chicago University Press, 1947), and *The Hays Office* by Raymond Moley (Indianapolis, Bobbs-Merrill, 1945). There is also the dry, legally authoritative *Film Censors and the Law* by Neville March Hunnings (London, Allen and Unwin, 1967).

Sternberg, Josef von, *Fun in a Chinese Laundry* (New York, Macmillan, 1965; London, Secker and Warburg, 1966). Extremely idiosyncratic autobiography by one of Hollywood's most difficult personalities, an important artist who had nothing but contempt for his employers and most of his contemporaries.

Tyler, Parker, *Magic and Myth of the Movies* (New York, Henry Holt, 1947). A remarkable study of the mythic, hallucinatory and unconscious impact of Hollywood pictures; the book that Gore Vidal's Myra Breckinridge kept at her bedside.

Tyler, Parker, *The Three Faces of the Film* (New York, A. S. Barnes, 1960 and 1967; London, Thomas Yoseloff, 1967). A follow-up to *Magic and Myth* extending the field and treating European and Asian cinema, and with a particularly good chapter on 'Hollywood as a Universal Church'.

Walker, Alexander, *The Celluloid Sacrifice* (London, Michael Joseph, 1966; New York, Hawthorn Books, 1967). A sharp examination, full of insight of 'Some Aspects of Sex in the Movies', mainly the making of Hollywood's goddesses. The section on censorship has been brought up to date with a lengthy postscript on recent developments for a paperback edition baldly re-titled *Sex in the Movies* (London and New York, Penguin Books, 1968).

Of the numerous Hollywood novels the best in my opinion is Nathanael West's *The Day of the Locust* (1939) which concerns people on the fringe of the industry. (West himself worked mainly on low budget pictures at Republic.) In the text and biographical notes I have mentioned several works of fiction that deal with the tycoons, of which the most important and running West close for literary quality are of course Fitzgerald's *The Last Tycoon* and Budd Schulberg's *What Makes Sammy Run?* To these I would add *The Producer* by Richard Brooks (1951), a novel inspired by the career of the late Mark Hellinger for whom Brooks worked as a screenwriter. In addition to the excellent early story *Crazy Sunday,* Fitzgerald also wrote many Hollywood potboilers for *Esquire* magazine about the hack screenwriter Pat Hobby (collected as *The Pat Hobby Stories* in 1962), and Schulberg has also written several short stories about Hollywood, some of which are to be found in his collection *Some Faces in the Crowd* (1954). Michael Millgate has an interesting chapter on the Hollywood novel in his *American Social Fiction* (Edinburgh, Oliver and Boyd, 1964), and there are some reflections on the Hollywood novel in Leslie Fiedler's *Waiting for the End* (London, Jonathan Cape, 1965). Three excellent chapters on Fitzgerald and Hollywood are contained in Henry Dan Piper's admirable *F. Scott Fitzgerald: A Critical Portrait* (London, The Bodley Head, 1966).

The author and publishers are grateful to the many copyright-owners who have given their permission to quote from published material, among them the following: The Bodley Head, for passages from *The Last Tycoon* in *The Bodley Head Scott Fitzgerald*, Volume I; Faber and Faber Ltd, for lines from *The Cocktail Party;* Design Yearbook Ltd, for extracts from *Fritz Lang in America,* and A. D. Peters & Company for quotations from *The Public is Never Wrong.* The lines from *Pal Joey* are copyright Chappell & Co. Inc. 1952.

INDEX

References in italics are to illustrations, and those in bold type are to the biographical notes (pages 135-57)

165

Index

167

Index

Index

Index